# THE WORST OF RUGBY

**Patrick Kidd**

Violence and foul play in a hooligans' game played by gentlemen

**Patrick Kidd** has been a rugby lover since he was smuggled into Twickenham without a ticket at the age of five and watched Dusty Hare's one-man effort for England to repel the Irish invaders. A combination of short-sightedness, asthma and general lack of fitness meant that his playing career never went past the college second XV level, where he played as a weak prop, a short lock and a slow back-row forward depending on who hadn't shown up. He supports Blackheath, England and whoever is playing New Zealand in a World Cup.

# THE WORST OF RUGBY

### Patrick Kidd

Violence and foul play in a hooligans' game played by gentlemen

## The Worst of Rugby

*Violence and foul play in a hooligans' game played by gentlemen*

© 2009 Patrick Kidd

Patrick Kidd has asserted his rights in accordance with the Copyright, Designs and Patents Act 1988 to be identified as the author of this work.

**Publishing by:**

Pitch Publishing (Brighton) Ltd
A2 Yeoman Gate
Yeoman Way
Worthing BN13 3QZ
*Email:* info@pitchpublishing.co.uk
*Web:* www.pitchpublishing.co.uk

First published 2009.

2

13-digit ISBN: 9781905411429

**Getty Images:** Cover, pages: 9, 30–31, 74–75, 96–97, 118–119, 140–141, 184–185, 206–207, 228–229, 250–251, 272–273, 294–25, 316–317, 338, 340.

**Page layout, design and illustration:**

Luke Jefford & Associates
*Tel:* +44 (0) 1273 297 872
*Email:* luke.jefford@ntlworld.com

Printed in Malta. Manufacturing managed by Jellyfish Print Solutions Limited.

4

# Contents

# Introduction

The tale of Buck Shelford's shredded scrotum (see page 98) has always fascinated me. This gruesome but somehow absorbing story features everything that attracts some of us to rugby: rough play, a nasty injury and, above all, a player with the strength of character to return from adversity with barely a grumble.

It is the way that rugby players just get on with things that sets this wonderful sport apart from football. Opponents say that rugby is a violent game, one played by hooligans who should be gentlemen, but it trumps football every time for the way that violence is taken with equanimity. It is part of the game, but it isn't so important that anyone gets het up about it.

Give me someone who is thumped and gets up without complaint, merely determined to get revenge later in the match, over a footballer who, when tapped from behind by a trip that wouldn't have felled a mouse, rolls over and over, clutching the afflicted limb as if it had been struck with a lump hammer in an attempt to con a free kick out of the official that will probably be wasted anyway.

This book features some of the most flagrant acts of violence and the nastiest injuries that have occured on a rugby field. It also features skulduggery, streakers, corruption and confusion, as well as some of the most embarrassing defeats inflicted on teams.

We call it the "Worst of Rugby" but in a way this celebrates why we love the game. In every unexpected loss, there is triumph for the other side; from every calamity, teams emerge stronger; violence is met with violence; rules are there to be broken, but if you get caught you should admit your mistake and take the punishment.

Let us not forget that rugby began with a cheat. Young Master William Webb Ellis may have created a new game when he picked up the football and ran with it at Rugby School, but he will no doubt have received six of the best from his games master for disobeying the rules. Naturally, Webb Ellis went on to become a clergyman.

In fact, the tale of Webb Ellis's breach of the rules may have been overplayed. There is no evidence that he committed the foul: the story emerged only after his death. But the fact that rugby has been happy for more than a century to proclaim that it developed from chaeting says much about the game. A plaque at Rugby School commemorates the place where Webb Ellis did the dirty "with a fine disregard for the rules of football". We have continued to appreciate a fine disregard for rules ever since.

# CHAPTER ONE

# The Worst Acts of Violence

# 1  Back assaults referee

**R**ugby players can be rough and tough and crude but the one thing they are invariably is courteous to the referee. Decisions are normally accepted with little dissent, the man with the whistle is usually called "sir" and violence against the official is strictly forbidden.

Tell that to Neil Back, the Leicester flanker, who was given a six-month ban in 1996 after he shoved Steve Lander, the referee, to the ground at the end of the Pilkington Cup final. Back's odd defence was that he had mistaken Lander for Andy Robinson, the Bath back row, who had been repeatedly standing offside. That the man he assaulted had just blown the whistle to end the game seemed to pass Back by.

It is doubly surprising that Back should have misidentified Lander as the referee had only a minute earlier awarded Bath a penalty try which, once converted, gave them a 16-15 win. It was Bath's tenth win in 13 years and Leicester were understandably hacked off at being the bridesmaids again. Back refused to return to the pitch to collect his runners-up medal.

Many felt that Back should have been banned for life. Jeff Probyn, the former England prop and a member of the RFU committee, said that the RFU should have made an example of him.

"If he doesn't feel he's lucky, he should," Probyn said. "The excuse that he thought it was Robinson doesn't wash. He has no right to assault a player, either."

As it was, the six-month ban was applied from the moment of the ruling, which meant that a fair portion of it was spent during the summer break. Back ended up missing only ten weeks of the next season as well as a Barbarians match against Japan. It did not affect his international career and seven years later all sins were forgotten as Back formed part of England's winning World Cup side.

# Mahoni stamps out of World Cup

I f Tonga had had as little discipline as Neil Back (see previous page), Steve Lander would have been flung to the floor a year earlier. Lander was the referee who sent Feleti Mahoni off in their World Cup pool match against France in Pretoria for stamping on an opponent's head.

The offence in the 68th minute spoilt what had been a promising and thoroughly committed start for the South Seas side against France. In the first half hour, Tonga had won 70 per cent of the possession and they were only six points behind at the interval. If only they had had a decent kicker, they could even have been in front. Sateki Tu'ipulotu missed six of his seven penalty goal attempts.

As often happens, it was the concession of a try, making a win just that little bit harder, that made the nervous tension and aggression spill over. Thierry Lacroix scored France's first try and moments later Mahoni was caught for stamping on the head of Philippe Benetton as the France back row lay on the floor at the base of a ruck. It was a moment of foolish exuberance, but it cost Tonga a man. Strangely, video replays suggested later that it may not have even been Mahoni's boot that raked Benetton's head in the ruck, although it was certainly a Tongan who did the deed. Mahoni was the man who got the two-month ban and an early flight home.

Facing 14 men, France relaxed and ran in three tries in the final ten minutes. Tonga had a consolation try in injury time, for Ipolito Fenukitau, that received the biggest cheer of the night. Mana Otai, the Tonga captain, had said before that match that his side were not prepared to be anyone's doormat. Just a shame that Mahoni (or someone) decided to use Benetton as their doormat.

# 3 Tonga join hundred club

**M**ahoni (see previous page) was the first of three Tongans to be sent off in the World Cup. The pool match between England and Tonga in 1999 was tipped to be a close-fought affair but although there was plenty of fighting the scoreline was anything but close after Tonga received a red card and two yellows in the space of three minutes before half-time.

A few days after Samoa had beaten Wales 38-31, Tonga were hoping to provide another night to remember for the Pacific. They fought back well from 11-0 down after 12 minutes to 11-7 and then 17-10, but there were already signs that the game was about to spill over with Wayne Erickson having words with Elisi Vunipola'a, the Tonga captain, after persistent infringements by his forwards.

With ten minutes to go in the first half, Phil Greening crashed over to extend England's lead to 24-10 and the frustration clearly got to the Pacific islanders. Matt Perry, the England full back, went up to catch a high ball and was taken out in mid-air by Isi Tapueluelu, causing him to land on his neck and shoulder. Although Perry was able to get up and walk, the tackle was highly dangerous and Phil Vickery's aggressive reaction was understandable. What was inexcusable was the action of Ngalu Taufo'ou, who smashed Richard Hill, the flanker, in the side of the head with his forearm during a mass brawl.

The Tonga prop was sent off, while Tapueluelu and Vickery received yellow cards. Within a couple of minutes, David Edwards, the Tonga flanker, joined them in a packed sin-bin after throwing yet another punch. Half-time could not come soon enough.

It was all jolly fun but without a full XV Tonga could not compete with England. They conceded two tries in stoppage time in the first half and then caved in completely in the second. England scored nine tries in the second period and won 101-10. Tonga should have learnt a lesson that violence never pays, but eight years later they suffered their third sending off at a World Cup when Hale T Pole was dismissed against Samoa.

# 4  Not a Wiese move

**T**hese days Kobus Wiese is a mild-mannered former rugby player, who owns a restaurant and a coffee shop and earns some extra cash from regaling crowds with humorous anecdotes as an after-dinner speaker. In South Africa he is still regarded as a hero for playing his part in the 1995 World Cup win.

In Wales, however, Wiese is Bogeyman No 1 for his role just a couple of months after the World Cup when he threw a haymaker that laid out Derwyn James, the Wales lock, near the start of their Test at Ellis Park. It was the first international match to be played in the bright new professional era, but Wiese was quick to show that all the old amateur habits of skulduggery and thuggery had not disappeared.

The bookmakers were predicting that the world champions would comfortably win by more than 70 points, but Wales showed that they had other ideas in mind when Mark Bennett, the Cardiff flanker, scored in the third minute. South Africa did not like their dominance challenged and Wiese, who had lost two lineouts to his opposite number already, decided that the best way to counter James was to thump him on the back of the head.

It wasn't the only act of violence. In the last minute of an ill-tempered match, which South Africa won 40-11, Garin Jenkins showed that Welshmen could punch hard too as he knocked Joost van der Westhuizen to the ground. The difference was that Jenkins's offence was seen by the referee and he was sent off, while Wiese escaped immediate punishment.

His just deserts came later when the Wales management cited him and, on reviewing the TV evidence, it was decided to fine Wiese £9,000 and suspend him for 30 days. He was the first player to be fined for ill discipline, although given that he had just signed a professional contract worth £140,000 over three years it was probably not too much of a punishment.

# 5  Loe makes a smash

**I**n a fairly packed field, Richard Loe, a prop from Canterbury who played 49 Tests for New Zealand, has a reputation as the dirtiest player in All Blacks history. It was burnished in one golden fortnight in 1992 when Loe smashed an Australian rival's skull and then broke another Australian's nose in the next match.

In the first Test of the Bledisloe Cup series in Sydney, Loe survived calls to be disciplined after a clash with Sam Scott-Young that left the Australia No 8 needing 15 stitches in his head. Two weeks later, Australia again demanded action after Loe's elbow somehow connected with Paul Carozza's nose, causing blood to spray over the diminutive wing's jersey. The odd thing was that Carozza wasn't even in action at that time: he was lying on the turf exhausted after scoring a try. For some reason neither the referee nor the touch judge saw Loe's unorthodox method of congratulating a rival.

In both matches, Loe got away without punishment but his actions somehow galvanised the Australians, who won the first Test 16-15 and then the second 19-17. Carozza even scored a second try to secure the win and no doubt make his throbbing nose hurt less.

Loe was later suspended from rugby for gouging in a domestic match, but he returned for the 1995 World Cup, his third, and continued to deserve his nickname as "The Enforcer". There is a delightful tale that in a state match shortly after the Carozza incident one Australian bravely decided to "sort him out" and hit him with one of those late tackles that make women weep and men turn their eyes away. As Loe shakily got to his feet, his first words to the referee were "Don't send him off". At that point, the attacker began to beg for an early shower.

In another story – and these may be apocryphal – a stern critic of the New Zealand team, who had been faxing complaints to the All Blacks hotel, was telephoned by Loe who asked him bluntly if he had a problem. "No, no problem at all," was the petrified response.

# 6  Lewis Moody makes history

**T**here is standing up for your mate and then there is wanton violence. Lewis Moody, the England flanker, went a step too far in supporting Mark Cueto in 2005 after the England wing was tackled in the air by Alesana Tuilagi, his Samoa opposite number at Twickenham, and landed on his head. By wading in with his fists, Moody made history: the first Englishman to be sent off at Headquarters and only the fourth in total.

Cueto hadn't taken too kindly to being dumped on his bonce and when he tried to argue with Tuilagi, the Samoan punched him, sparking Moody's reprisal and a general brawl. In the end the referee settled for only two red cards, one for Moody and one for Tuilagi.

Ironically they were club team-mates at Leicester and no doubt their reunion on the training ground the next week must have been a bit awkward.

Andy Robinson, the England head coach, said that Moody had merely been trying to make peace when he struck Tuilagi with a flurry of punches. Michael Jones, the Samoa coach, pointed out that Moody had run in with his dukes up and struck Tuilagi on the back of the head.

Moody, who has a reputation for acting first and thinking second, had already served a six-week ban that season for punching an opponent in a second-team club match against Leeds and he could have been banned for 12 months. Instead, he got off with only a nine-week suspension, which meant that he would be eligible to play for England in the following spring's Six Nations Championship. Tanner Vili, the Samoa fly half, was also cited and received a two-week ban for a high tackle on the unfortunate Cueto earlier in the match. For all their aggression, Samoa were hardly in the game. England won 40-3.

# 7  Bracken's painful debut

**J**amie Joseph, the former All Blacks flanker, is now making his way as a respected coach of Wellington, but no doubt his young players have heard of **the** time when the boss gutlessly reduced an England debutant's ankle to pulp.

Joseph was playing his thirteenth Test and was already a canny enough flanker to know that his job was to try and get away with the odd bit of GBH while the referee wasn't watching, so when he saw the tempting right ankle of Kyran Bracken sticking out of a ruck just 75 seconds into the game, Joseph made sure that his boot came down hard upon it and gave Bracken a debut to remember. It probably helped that Bracken was a fresh-faced youth with a public schoolboy quiff and a plummy voice, the sort of player that New Zealanders have always liked to bring down a peg or two.

When Bracken was shown the video afterwards, he diplomatically said that "what happened could have been avoided". He had soldiered on for the rest of the game, not wanting to come off in his first match, but he was put on crutches immediately afterwards and ended up being out of action for three months. His ankle remained weak, although it did not stop him from becoming a successful celebrity ice skater.

Buoyed by the resilience of their scrum half, England were lifted a gear or three and pulled off a surprising 15-9 win, with Jon Callard, another debutant, kicking four penalty goals. New Zealand never made public if Joseph was disciplined.

Joseph, the son of a tough New Zealand Maori player and coach, was always going to be a bruiser. In his first All Blacks trial, he decided it would be a bright idea to punch Mike Brewer, the captain at the time, at his first lineout. He won selection on the back of it.

# 8  Nice one. Cyril

Cyril Brownlie's name is not as well known now as it once was. For 42 years he was the only man to have been sent off in an international. Indeed there were only two red cards issued in the 50 years after Brownlie was given his marching orders at Twickenham by Albert Freethy, a retired first-class cricketer from Swansea.

The match on January 3, 1925, was New Zealand v England and a record crowd of 60,000, which included the Prince of Wales, had come to Twickenham to see if the home team could stop the team that would be given the epithet The Invincibles. To that point New Zealand had won the first 27 matches of their northern hemisphere tour and had kept the other side off the scoreboard in 13 of them. Wales had been brushed aside 19-0, Ireland 6-0.

Yet perhaps the All Blacks sensed that England might be a tougher proposition and needed some respect drummed into them. From the start there was scrapping at the scrummage. Freethy issued four warnings, two to each side, before the match had barely got going and announced that if he had to issue a fifth then he was not afraid to send someone off. The moment came with the match not even ten minutes old.

Freethy blew his whistle again and said that he had seen Brownlie, a lock whose brother Maurice was also in the team, deliberately kick an opponent lying on the ground. Brownlie was sent off for an early bath, not that it stopped New Zealand from eking out a tough 17-11 win. Maurice Brownlie scored their final try. The Invincibles went on to win their five remaining matches of the tour, including a 30-6 demolition of France.

Four decades later, Colin Meads, another New Zealander, became the second man to get a red card, for dangerous play against Scotland. The *Daily Telegraph* reported that "For one with Meads's world-wide reputation for robust play, this was rather like sending a burglar to prison for a parking offence."

# 9  Devereux does time for punch

**F**ebruary 1996 was a good and a bad month for rugby players called Devereux. On February 21, John Devereux, who had been capped for Wales in both codes, became the first professional rugby player to be committed to both sports at once, playing union for Sale in the winter and league for Widnes in the summer. A day later, Simon Devereux (no relation) was sentenced to nine months in prison for throwing a punch during a match.

It happened in a second-team game for Gloucester against Rosslyn Park. It was the sort of senseless act that happens in rugby from time to time, but the 27-year-old lock's assault on Jamie Cowie, which broke the flanker's jaw in three places, had more serious effects than previously handed down to assailants.

"Warnings have been given to all sportsmen, particularly in rugby, that unlawful punching cannot be tolerated," said the judge. It caused shockwaves in the sport, but made players and coaches realise that the consequences they now faced were different in the days of professionalism, when a willfully-thrown punch could end a career (Cowie was out for eight months) and cost money.

Gloucester fans thought that Devereux was being made an example. "If he'd been playing for Harlequins it would have been a different story," one said. They organised a whip-round to raise money for his family while he was inside. Lawyers argued that rugby players had in effect accepted that sometimes they might get punched as part of the job. Certainly punches still get thrown, yet players do not go to jail.

Devereux continued to play for Gloucester after his release. He broke his leg while playing in 1998 and ended his career at Worcester two years later. He later worked for the local BBC station.

# 10

## War-War is Jaw-Jaw for Price

**G**raham Price was that rarity, a Wales legend who instead of being born in the Valleys was brought forth in Egypt. However, having swapped the desert for Monmouth, Price was soon turned into the very model of a gritty Welsh prop forward and by 1978 was as crucial to the Wales cause as Gareth Edwards or Phil Bennett.

He had played in two grand slam-winning sides and toured New Zealand with the Lions in 1977. He had played his part in Wales's 1975 win over Australia in Cardiff, a year in which he even had had the temerity against France to run in a try from 70 yards out. He was, in other words, a prime target for the Australia pack when they played Wales in Sydney.

In the third minute of the game, as Wales tried to

defend against a high short kick by Paul McLean from a scrum, Price sustained a blow to the head from behind by Steve Finnane, his opposing loose-head. The punch shattered his jaw in two places. Photos of Price's bloodied face startled fans of both sides, but Price was, as you would expect, matter-of-fact about the incident. "He was just trying to intimidate me," he said. "But he caught me coming out of a scrum with my jaw at its most vulnerable – open and gasping for air."

Clive Rowlands, Price's manager, was less restrained. As Price recovered in hospital, Rowlands made a passionate speech at a reception after the game – backed by the Australian management – saying: "I have no wish to cause offence, but if I have a complaint to make I'll make it. I will never condone thuggery."

Even today Price is asked about the incident and his reply is always the same: these things happen, it is the law of the jungle out there and acts of violence will happen in rugby. Rowlands may not have condoned thuggery, but as a player he was a poncey back. Forwards recognise that thuggery is just part of the game.

# CHAPTER TWO

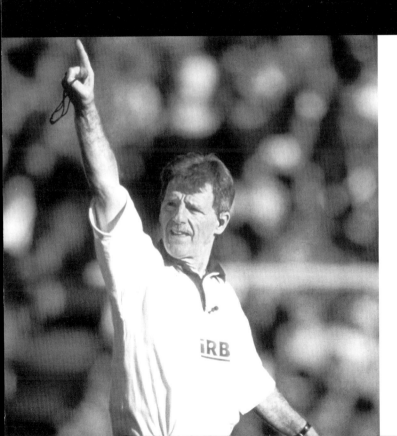

# The Worst of Referees

31

# 1 Derek Bevan and the gold watch

**F**or many, South Africa's march to the World Cup title on home soil in 1995 was a wonderful sight, especially when Nelson Mandela, wearing the Springboks jersey, embraced Francois Pienaar, the Afrikaner captain, after the victory in extra time of the final, a sign of how far the Rainbow Nation had come in such a short time.

Yet some felt that South Africa were lucky to get that far. Their semi-final against France was played on a near-flooded pitch in Durban after a 90-minute delay for the water to be swept aside and if lightning had returned during the first half or if the rain that had thudded down all day had increased to make the conditions wholly unplayable then, under the rules, the abandoned game would have been given to France on account of their superior disciplinary record.

It was an odd rule, but you can understand why Derek Bevan, the referee from Wales, did not want to reach that point. Which referee would want to knock a home side out of their own World Cup on account of the weather? Nonetheless, Bevan was to have a fatal say in the destination of the match.

South Africa led 10-6 at half-time

and were 19-15 up with 15 minutes remaining when France took up possession on their goal-line. First France were denied what appeared to be a perfectly good try when Christophe Deylaud lofted a kick that was dropped by Andre Joubert, the Springboks full back, and Abdelatif Benazzi slid in to take the catch and coast for the line. Bevan, in the days before video replays, ruled that he was stopped just short. If he was then it was by inches.

Then, as the clock ticked down, France had a series of five-metre scrums, two of which collapsed and, after the ball came out of another scrum, South African defenders pounced on the carrier and killed the ball. A brave man would have given a penalty try against them. Mr Bevan wasn't a brave man.

That was his call and he took some flak for it. But worse was to come in the post-tournament banquet when Louis Luyt, the bullish head of South African rugby, decided to present a gold watch to Bevan, calling him the most wonderful referee in the world. "It was something I could have done without," Bevan said later. "It could be misconstrued."

# Bob Deans denied by Dallas

In the entire history of rugby union there have been many contentious decisions that have turned matches, but one will still spark debate in pubs from Aberystwyth to Auckland despite the fact that the man at the centre of the controversy has been dead for more than a century.

It was mid-December 1905 and New Zealand were nearing the end of their first official tour of the northern hemisphere. Having beaten Scotland (12-7), Ireland (15-0) and England (also 15-0), they came to Cardiff Arms Park to play Wales with a grand slam in their sights. It is fair to claim that these original All Blacks were the most successful touring side in any sport. Having begun with a 55-4 win over Devon, it would be six more matches before another side scored a point against them. Over the course of that tour, they scored 976 points and conceded only 59; they won 35 matches and lost one.

But it is that one that got away in Cardiff that still rankles. Teddy Morgan, the London Welsh left wing, had already got up the noses of the New Zealanders by leading the 47,000-strong crowd in a chorus of *Land of My Fathers* in response to the haka war dance. Ten minutes before half-time, Morgan scored a try that gave Wales a 3-0 lead and so it stayed until in the dying minutes Bob Deans, the New Zealand centre, crossed the line to give his side the chance of winning with a conversion.

Just one flaw: by the time the Scottish referee, John Dallas, caught up with play, Deans had been yanked back in front of the line by the Wales defenders and Dallas ruled that he had been tackled short. Deans was furious, telling the *Daily Mail:* "I grounded the ball six inches over the line. Some of the Welsh players admit the try."

Dallas was pilloried afterwards, with George Dixon, the New Zealand manager, saying: "No referee who is commonly 30 or so yards behind the play can be classed A1." But the decision and the result stood. Three years later, Deans died after appendix surgery. He is said to have been protesting about the try on his death bed.

# 3

# Jonathan Kaplan's slow-running watch

**R**ugby union, for now, still allows the referee some leeway in deciding when a match is over. The clocks in many stadiums now stop when the referee signals a break in play, so that everyone in the ground knows how much time should be left, but technically it is still up to the referee rather than a hooter to end the game.

In 2000, Jonathan Kaplan, a South African referee, angered New Zealand fans who felt that they had been denied a sure victory by his mistake. Having lost the Bledisloe Cup to Australia in 1998, Todd Blackadder's All Blacks won the first match of their home-and-away series 39-35 in Sydney, meaning that they needed to win in Wellington to regain the trophy. With New

Zealand leading 23-21 and regulation time expired, Kaplan was asked how long was remaining and replied by holding up two fingers and saying "two".

Not unreasonably, New Zealand felt that meant they had two minutes to survive, so they were surprised when a further five minutes elapsed before Australia were given a penalty attempt, which John Eales slotted over to give Australia a one-point win. Kaplan left the field under a hail of plastic bottles from All Blacks fans, but said that he had no regrets and that New Zealand had been wasting time at lineouts, which had resulted in the extra time being added. "I blew it as I saw it," he said. New Zealand fans certainly felt he had blown it.

Seven years later, Kaplan's time-keeping was again criticised when he allowed enough minutes of extra time in the World Cup pool match between Canada and Japan for Japan to score a converted try and draw the match. He later said that the stadium and television clocks had not been stopped correctly during breaks in play.

# 4  Paddy O'Brien loses the plot

**N**o wonder Paddy O'Brien, now the head of referees at the International Rugby Board, is defensive of his officials who make mistakes (see Wayne Barnes entry in The Worst of the World Cup): he has received his own fair share of criticism, notably in his first World Cup, in 1999. France were the beneficiaries.

France and Fiji had both qualified from their pool when they met in the final match in Toulouse, but the prize for winning was a bye in the first knockout round. The losers would have to play England. Although France were at home, no one thought they were guaranteed a win. Fiji had been slightly more impressive in beating Canada and Namibia than France had.

The simple fact is that France won 28-19, but the victory was only certain when Christophe Dominici scored three minutes into stoppage time and France would not have led if, ten minutes earlier, they had not been awarded a contentious penalty try after eight consecutive scrums on the Fiji line. Many felt that it had been the French who infringed, not least Greg Smith, the Fiji hooker, who said: "We were robbed. Being in the front row I know a hell of a lot more about what's going on than the referee."

O'Brien's biggest mistakes came in the first half, however, with a string of contentious decisions, including three yellow cards against Fiji, which even the French players admitted were for imagined reasons. The worst error came when Ifereimi Tawake, the Fiji flanker, scored what appeared to be a legitimate try, but O'Brien called back play for what he saw as a knock-on in a tackle by Fiji. The rest of the stadium and those watching on TV saw the ball spilt instead by a Frenchman. He, after all, had been the one holding the ball when the tackle was made. To his credit, O'Brien later admitted: "I lost the plot."

# 5  Crowe croaks on home soil

**N**ew Zealand were on a roll in the late 1960s, with only one defeat in five years (and that by three points against the Springboks), but with the clock ticking down in their match against Australia in Brisbane in 1968 and the home side leading 18-14 it appeared that the Men in Black were heading for a rare loss. Up stepped a local referee to break Australian hearts and allow the New Zealand run to continue.

New Zealand were making a final desperate attack in the last two minutes. Bill Davis, their centre, kicked the ball into the Australia in-goal area and would have given chase had he not been brought down immediately after the kick by Barry Honan, the Australia defender. It was probably a penalty offence, but three points would not have been enough for New Zealand to win. Fortunately for them, the referee,

Kevin Crowe, blew his whistle and ran under the posts to award a penalty try, then worth three points plus a conversion for two, which Fergie McCormick made to give the All Blacks a 19-18 win.

Naturally, there was uproar at this seemingly harsh decision and by an Aussie too! Crowe and his touch judges needed a police escort off the pitch. They were taken to the referee's changing room, which was also the groundsman's shed, where they hid among the mowers and shovels as an angry mob battered on the door.

Crowe later claimed that he had awarded the penalty try not for the hit on Davis but for a separate tackle off the ball by Alan Cardy on Grahame Thorne, the New Zealand wing, during the move. Crowe claimed that Thorne, not Davis, would have been able to run on and score the try. He even asked Cardy at a press conference why he had hit Thorne and was told "I had to stop the bastard somehow", but the Australian press were only interested in what they saw as a harsh penalty try against Honan. None of them could recall even seeing Thorne being taken out. It remains one of their most frustrating defeats.

# Kinsey tames the Lions

**I**an McGeechan's book on the 1993 Lions tour to New Zealand, for which he was the head coach, was rightly called *So Close to Glory*. His side won the second Test 20-7 and although they were heavily beaten in the final match they could have won the series if the first Test had been 20-18 in their favour, rather than against.

That they lost the match was due to two contentious decisions by the Australian referee, Brian Kinsey, one in the first minute of the game and one in the last. "They meant that we lost a match I felt we could have won comfortably," McGeechan wrote. At the start of the match, Grant Fox, the New Zealand fly half, sent up a high kick that dropped towards the England line. Ieuan Evans, the Wales wing, leapt up to catch the ball and as he came back to earth was enveloped in a tackle by Frank Bunce. Welshman and All Black rolled over the line together but although the TV replays (not called on in those days) showed that Evans never let go of the ball, Kinsey awarded a try to New Zealand. It was noted that he was farther from the action at the time than most of the players. At the very least it should have been a New Zealand five-metre scrum. Many thought it should be a Lions drop-out.

Still, the Lions regrouped and with Gavin Hastings, the captain, scoring six penalty goals, they led 18-17 as the match neared its conclusion. Then up stepped Kinsey to have his say again. New Zealand had the ball, but Dean Richards made a big hit on Bunce and turned the All Black, who had no option but to release the ball. Players from both sides bundled on top of it – one New Zealander in fact stepping several feet over the ball – before Kinsey blew his whistle and penalised the Lions for holding on to the ball. Fox converted the chance and New Zealand won by two points.

As Hastings said afterwards, the decision did not make sense. "Why would he be holding the ball in that position at that time?" he asked. Dewi Morris, the scrum half, simply gaped open-mouthed and in anger at the ineptitude. If looks could kill, Morris would still be inside.

# 7 Hill delivers victory to England

**G**oogle the name Rowland Hill and you'll find plenty of entries on the Victorian social reformer who invented the prepaid postal stamp, truly one of the great benefits for civilisation (until e-mail came along anyway). Twenty years after that Hill died, in 1889, another Rowland Hill put his stamp on rugby history with an extremely partisan display of refereeing that delivered England a first-class victory over the New Zealand Natives touring side.

This Rowland Hill was secretary of the Rugby Football Union as well as the man with the whistle for the match at Blackheath in southeast London. Perhaps he was conscious that the New Zealanders had won their previous seven games, including a comprehensive win against Ireland; perhaps he was a little biased towards the home side; or perhaps he was just incompetent. Certainly he made a lot of curious decisions that benefited the home side.

Twice in the first half the ball was kicked behind the New Zealand line and touched down by one of their players, which should have resulted in a scrum, only for Harry Bedford, the

England forward, to run in and touch the ball down again and be given a try each time by Hill. That gave England a 2-0 half-time lead with tries only counting for one point in those days (fortunately for the New Zealanders, neither try was converted for two more points), but worse was to come at the start of the second half.

Andrew Stoddart, the future England cricket captain, lost his shorts in a tackle and as he was restoring his modesty the New Zealanders stood by idly. Play should have stopped, but Frank Evershed, the England prop, picked up the ball and cheekily put it over the New Zealand line. Hill awarded the try, to the astonishment of the New Zealanders, three of whom walked off the field and refused to continue. England won 7-0.

The matter didn't end there. The RFU, of whom Hill, remember, was secretary, demanded that an apology should be given for the insults to the referee. He even dictated the wording of the apology. There was no official farewell for the Natives when they returned to New Zealand. It was not England's finest hour.

# 8

# Simmonds forgets the rules

**E**ven the best of referees can have a sudden brain-freeze and even on the biggest of occasions. Perhaps Gareth Simmonds was not the best of referees and the SWALEC Cup final in 1993 was not the biggest of occasions but Simmonds was on the international panel of officials and should have known better for his error that allowed Llanelli to win the cup for the third successive year.

Neath were the underdogs against the dominant Welsh club of the time. Llanelli had beaten Australia, the world champions, the previous season and in 1993 they did the league and cup double. But it was a close-run thing at Cardiff Arms Park. The match was tied at 18-18 with about a quarter of an hour to play when Llanelli were awarded a free kick. Rupert Moon, their captain, took it quickly and passed the ball to Emyr Lewis, who kicked a dropped goal that put Llanelli ahead.

The problem was that, according to the rules that had been brought in that season, Llanelli should not have been allowed to do that. The ball needed to touch an opponent first, a point that Paul Thorburn, the Neath and Wales full back, politely made to Simmonds, but although the referee admitted his mistake he said that he could not change his mind once it was given.

Neath were certainly unlucky. They also blamed Simmonds for allowing Llanelli's second try after Nigel Davies had illegally played the ball on the ground after a tackle. But to blame the referee would be to fail to acknowledge the magnificence of Ieuan Evans, the supreme wing in Wales at the time, who scored two tries for Llanelli in the final to take his haul in that year's cup competition to a record 40 tries. Truly a feat worth recording over any referee's hiccup.

# 9

# Neath get the rub of the green

Llanelli may have felt piqued by Neath's complaining about losing the 1993 Welsh Cup final (see previous page), given that when the same two sides had met in the cup final four years earlier the referee's mistakes had benefited the Neath men.

Actually it was more the generosity of the referee, Les Peard, rather than his errors that helped Neath. It came in the first half when he decided to send Mark Jones, the Neath No 8, to the sin-bin for ten minutes after stamping on the face of Laurence Delaney, the Llanelli and Wales prop. The offence happened quite openly, in view of the referee, and many expected

Peard to reach for the red card. Instead he gave Jones a reprieve and when the back row returned in the second half he shored up the Neath scrum, which had appeared in danger of buckling while he was away.

As Llanelli, behind 14-13 in the closing minutes, pressed for a winning score, Neath even won a scrum against the head, which they would surely not have done if they had only seven men in their pack. Jones also played his role in helping Neath to dominate the lineout. Time and again, Llanelli pushed and probed to find a way. Time and again Neath kept them out. In such a tight match, they must have been delighted to have been playing with a full XV. It was their first Welsh Cup win since the inaugural tournament, in 1972. Llanelli were the opponents on that day, too. Those two sides must have really got sick of each other.

# 10 Honiss forgets the rules

**P**aul Honiss may never have become a referee if it hadn't been for sustaining a concussion while playing rugby as a schoolboy. Ireland certainly praised whoever had laid out the teenaged Honiss after the New Zealand referee's kindness helped them to beat South Africa in 2004.

The error came from a procedural misunderstanding by Honiss, normally such a stickler on detail, in the first half. It was shaping up to be a rough match, as games involving South Africa usually are, and after one set-to, Honiss blew his whistle to award a penalty to Ireland, said "time off" to the television official and then called over the Springboks captain, John Smit, and asked him to have a word with his players about them coming off their feet at the ruck.

According to the laws, Honiss should then have blown his whistle a second time and said "time on" before letting play go ahead. Instead, Ronan O'Gara asked "Can I go?" and, on receiving a nod, took a quick tap-penalty instead of aiming at the sticks and ran through untouched as South Africa looked on amazed.

Nick Mallett, the former South Africa coach, called it "probably the worst decision I've seen". Andre Watson, a former South African referee, said it was "a terrible slip-up". Honiss, trying to deflect the criticism after the match, said it was the South Africans' fault for turning their backs on the opposition, although it could be argued that having told their captain to have a word with his players, it was fair enough that the Boks should have a quick huddle. Ireland won 17-12. Two years later, they again played South Africa at Lansdowne Road. Clearly whoever arranges the assignment of referees had a sense of humour as Honiss was again given the job. This time there was less controversy as Ireland won 32-15.

# CHAPTER THREE

# The Worst of Fans

# 1 Pieter Van Zyl

South Africa has never had a shortage of hard tacklers but they tend to wear better-fitting Springboks shirts than that sported by Pieter Van Zyl, an obese owner of a mining company from Potchefstroom, who played an unwelcome role early in the second half of South Africa's Tri-Nations match against New Zealand in Durban in 2002.

It had been a contentious match and many of the home fans were angered by a series of decisions against their side by the Irish referee, David McHugh. The Springboks had scored within the first two minutes through a try by Neil de Kock, the scrum half, but the All Blacks pulled five points back within three minutes with a try by Leon Macdonald and then went ahead when McHugh awarded them a penalty try after De Wet Barry almost decapitated Tana Umaga when the New Zealand centre had the line beckoning.

That was controversial enough but McHugh really enraged the 57,000-strong crowd when he ruled out Breyton Paulse's subsequent try for an obstruction. South Africa and New Zealand traded a try each before the break to leave the game intriguingly poised at 17-17 but clearly some fans were brooding during the interval.

The second half had barely begun when the galloping figure of the 18-stone Van Zyl was seen heading McHugh's way. Quite how he avoided a few hundred security officials is unclear. The referee was setting a scrum and had his back to his assailant, so wasn't prepared for Van Zyl's enormous hit, which dislocated his left shoulder. Not that Van Zyl came away unscathed; he was punched in the mouth by Richie McCaw, the All Blacks flanker.

Van Zyl was fined 10,000 rand for assault and banned from attending matches in South Africa. He showed no remorse and said it was the referee's fault for doing fans a disservice. "Fans like me is what rugby is about," he said. A spokesman for South Africa Rugby said the incident had damaged his country's reputation. "It just reinforces the image that people have of South Africa supporters being boorish brandy and coke drinkers," he said. New Zealand won the match 30-23 under a new referee.

# The Vodafone streak

**O**nly a week before Van Zyl's **moment of idiocy, the Tri-Nations had suffered** another pitch invasion, this time during the match between Australia and New Zealand in Sydney. New Zealand had to win to regain the Bledisloe Cup for the first time since 1997 and in a ding-dong game they had come back from 8-3 down at half-time to lead 14-8 in the final quarter, thanks to two penalty goals by Andrew Mehrtens and a try for Richie McCaw.

However, Mehrtens also missed a penalty late in the game that proved crucial. His attention was possibly distracted by two male streakers who ran on to the pitch wearing nothing but the red and white Vodafone logo painted on their backs. They ran up to the New Zealand fly half and circled him until they were collected by the security staff. A flustered Mehrtens then missed the kick. Australia came roaring back with a try for Mat Rogers and a last-minute penalty by Matt

Burke to win the game 16-14.

Streakers have long been a part of rugby and long may they remain so, but the incident was particularly embarrassing for the telecommunications company when their chief executive said that he had been given an inkling of what was about to happen.

Grahame Maher told police that he had been telephoned by someone called Brett before the game, saying that he was planning a stunt that would give Vodafone some publicity.

Although the specifics of the stunt were not mentioned, Maher agreed to pay any fine that was given to Brett.

Vodafone later agreed to pay about £30,000 to a campaign to reduce sports injuries as well as taking out full-page advertisements in New Zealand newspapers to apologise to their fans. To his credit, Justin Marshall, the All Blacks captain, didn't blame the invaders for the loss, while Mehrtens blamed the referee instead for awarding the late penalty to Australia.

# 3

# That wasn't in the programme

This one gets in because it is quite amusing, rather than anything too dastardly. It was a Saturday evening in December, 2007, and London Wasps, the previous year's Heineken Cup champions, were up against it in their quest to defend the title. Drawn in a tough pool with Munster, Clermont Auvergne and Llanelli Scarlets, Wasps had sneaked a one-point win at home to Munster but having lost away to Clermont needed to beat the French in the return leg at home in order to keep their hopes alive.

All looked good for the English club at first after they raced into a 22-0 lead, but Clermont bounced back and were 22-10 down when the fractious game boiled over. In the 58th minute, Jamie Cudmore, the Clermont flanker, was possibly kicked by Tim Payne, the Wasps prop, and retaliated in time-honoured fashion with fists flailing. At this point various players from both sides decided they would like a go, too, and a series of scuffles broke out.

Feeling left out in the crowd was Alan Black, a captain of Wasps in the early 1970s and now a committee member who had a day job working for the Rugby Football Union. He should have known better but something just snapped and Black, who was standing by a railing, leaned over and aimed a blow at the head of Martin Scelzo, the Clermont prop, with his rolled-up programme.

It was a fairly pathetic assault and in any case Black, 60, missed his target, clipping James Haskell, the Wasps back row, instead, but the reaction to his "assault" was almost as severe as that faced by Van Zyl (see page 54). Scelzo complained, Black apologised and after a disciplinary hearing he was given a one-year ban. Lawrence Dallaglio, the Wasps captain, made the most commonsense point in Black's defence, saying: "Let's get it into perspective. A guy throws six punches and gets yellow-carded whereas another guy hits someone with a programme. The incident has to be taken in the context of what happened previously – a guy had thrown a load of punches." It rather overshadowed the fact that a cracking game then developed, with Wasps clinging on to win 25-24.

# Bath take exuberance too far

The *Daily Telegraph* did not pull its punches in assessing the premature celebrations of the Bath crowd near the end of the John Player Cup final in 1987. The *Telegraph's* correspondent called the "thousands" of supporters who twice invaded the Twickenham pitch when Bath scored near the end of the match against Wasps "a rabble" and "so-called supporters" who committed "the worst scenes of undiluted yobbery ever witnessed at the ground". They certainly had a crucial impact on the game as after their second invasion, the match was abandoned by the referee, Fred Howard, with three minutes remaining to be played. Bath led 19-12 at that point, more than a try ahead under the scoring system at the time.

It was the beginning of the end of amateurism for rugby. The first World Cup would start a fortnight after this match and the rather arbitrary merit tables were about to be replaced by a more structured pyramid league system. Players were still eight years away from getting paid for their hard work, however, and fans were still allowed to come on to the pitch at the end of a match to congratulate their heroes. The crucial words being "at the end of a match".

No doubt the Bath supporters were relieved that the match was turning their way. This was the fourth successive cup final they had appeared in and they were going for a fourth win, but Wasps, whom they had beaten 25-17 in the previous season, were controlling the game with ten minutes to go when Bath suddenly scored a try to take the lead, sparking the first invasion. Seven minutes later they scored again and this time the fans were less keen to clear off. Some even stole the match balls.

The referee had no option but to take the players off, but when he tried to resume play he found that some had assumed the match was over and swapped shirts with their opponents. There was little appetite to go out and finish so the match was abandoned and Bath declared the winners. The next day a group of MPs urged the RFU to step up its stewarding at Twickenham and so began the sad decline of interaction between fans and players.

# Flour power

The three-match series between New Zealand and South Africa in 1981 was a humdinger, with a finale known as much for exciting events off the field as on it. Rarely can international sides have played out a match while being dive-bombed from the air, even if the assailants were dropping nothing more dangerous than flour.

New Zealand had won the first Test of the series in Christchurch 14-9, but they had lost in Wellington 24-12 making the deciding match in Auckland, watched by 50,000 people, crucial. It would turn out to be the final rugby match between these giants of the sport for 11 years as South Africa's rugby players soon followed their cricketers into the sporting wilderness because of the apartheid boycott.

The home side went ahead 16-3 in the first half through tries by Gary Knight and Stu Wilson, but the Springboks came roaring back and so did the anti-apartheid airborne assailants in a light aircraft who began an hour-long period of bombarding the pitch with bags of flour, propaganda leaflets and smoke canisters. One of these canisters ignited on the touchline, belching red fumes that got in the eyes of the players, while poor Knight was hit on the head by one of the sacks of flour. "I've heard of Bread of Heaven," he said, clearly thinking he was playing Wales, "but this was ridiculous."

The protest, for all the worthiness of its intentions, spoilt what was a thrilling conclusion. As the match went into injury time Ray Mordt, the South Africa wing, scored his third try of the half to make the scores level at 22-22, but Naas Botha, normally such an assured kicker, missed the conversion that would have won the game. Instead, there was just time for New Zealand to move the ball downfield and Allan Hewson kicked the ball over to secure a win. South Africa have now not beaten the All Blacks in Auckland since 1937.

# 6 How many tickets did you say you want?

These days the Scottish rugby union is sadly pessimistic about selling out Murrayfield even for the biggest of matches, but it wasn't always like this. In 1975, so many people showed up for the Five Nations match against Wales that several thousand who had arrived in hope of getting tickets on the gate were turned away. The ground had a capacity of 80,000 at the time, yet it is estimated that 104,000 squeezed in (ah, those were the days, pre-Hillsborough, when grounds had standing areas and they would make every effort to fit extra people in).

There was a certain air of anticipation in Edinburgh that afternoon for the opening match of the Five Nations. Two years earlier Scotland had beaten Wales 10-9 at Murrayfield in a tournament where everyone won their home matches and lost their away games. Scotland had been pipped to the title a year later by Ireland, who had won their crucial game 9-6, and there was a growing feeling that 1975 could be Scotland's year.

They had not won the tournament

outright since 1938, having held it jointly with Wales in 1964 as well as the five-way tie in 1973, but at last had a side worth pinning your hopes on, which included the likes of Andy Irvine at full back, Ian McGeechan at fly half and Gordon Brown in the second row. They had beaten Ireland and lost to France by only a point, but the tournament was wide open so long as they could beat Wales, who were a bit useful in the 1970s.

Win they did, 12-10, but there were tens of thousands of Scots who were disgruntled that they hadn't quite seen the match. As well as those who couldn't even get into the ground, there were many who were allowed to sit on the grass behind the in-goal areas and later complained that they had been banned from standing up and so couldn't see the action. The SRU issued an apology for underestimating the interest, but who really cared? Scotland had beaten Wales and were on their way! Sadly, they lost their last game to England away, 7-6, which cost them another share of the title. It would be nine more years before they won it again.

# 7 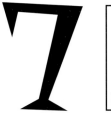   Excess fans
hosed down

**A**lmost 40 years before the 104,000 who turned up to watch Scotland at Murrayfield (previous page), police also had to get tough with the extra enthusiastic fans who went to Cardiff Arms Park to watch Wales against Ireland in 1936. It was a title decider but those who walked to the ground must have been praying for a more exciting match than the previous one in Cardiff two months earlier, when Wales had an unappetising 0-0 draw against England (a scoreline that would only happen twice more in the next 70 years of Home Nations rugby).

Wales had got themselves back on track with a 13-3 win away to Scotland and with France absent because of a row over professionalism – and England surprisingly toothless against Ireland despite the presence of

Alexander Obolensky, the dashing Russian prince on the wing who had scored two tries as England beat New Zealand two months earlier – it all came down to Wales v Ireland for the title. No wonder there was some interest.

With two hours to go until kick-off and a record 70,000 spectators already inside the Arms Park, the authorities decided that the ground had reached its safe limit. They politely told the fans to go away but with there being only 12,000 TV sets in the whole of Britain that year (and probably none in Cardiff pubs) and radio still rather scratchy, their decision to stay was understandable.

In fact, the fans locked out did not just decide to stay: they rushed the gates in protest, at which the police decided to turn fire hoses on them. It made little difference: soaking wet, they burst through the barricades and spilt on to the pitch, standing 15 men deep on the touchlines. One man was killed in the crush. And those who got to watch the match were hardly rewarded. Ireland won the game and the title by the paltry score of a penalty goal to nothing.

# 8  The worst protest?

The political situation in South Africa enflamed passions, especially among students in the 1960s. In 1969, the New Zealand group Halt All Racist Tours was created to protest against South Africa's policy of refusing to host mixed-race teams. South Africa had already been suspended by Fifa and were about to be thrown out of the International Cricket Conference. Tempers ran high whenever South Africa took part in sport, so when word went around that there would be a mass protest at Twickenham when Oxford University played South Africa in 1969, the authorities decided to be ready for them.

More than 400 policemen were at the ground and three stands of the stadium were closed off. A dozen Black Maria police wagons were parked outside the stadium, ready to cart off the misbehaved, and plain-clothes policemen mingled with spectators. A detachment from Scotland Yard's Commando squad were even sent in. For once, the pitch was declared an out-of-bounds zone to fans and a pleading message over the loudspeaker told the crowd to "please leave all control to our friends the police".

It was certainly a thorough response to face down any violent protest. And what were the police met with? Hand-clapping. It turned out that demonstrators among the crowd of 12,000 numbered barely 300, split into three not particularly threatening groups. As well as clapping, they tried to shout Sieg Heil when South Africa marched on, but were drowned out by hearty applause. Perhaps this was a reflection of George Orwell's claim that the cause of British fascism would be set back a decade by a bomb under the West car park at Twickenham.

The match itself did more to dent apartheid South Africa's pride than any protest. Oxford, led by Chris Laidlaw, the former All Black on a Rhodes scholarship, beat the mighty Springboks 6-3.

# Brennan's
# Cantona moment

**O**ne of the funniest – or most shocking, depending on your mood at the time – interactions between a footballer and a fan happened at Crystal Palace in 1995 when Eric Cantona leapt into the crowd to show off his kung-fu skills. Twelve years later, rugby had its own Cantona moment when Trevor Brennan, a Dubliner who had played international rugby six years earlier but was now winding down his career at Toulouse, decided to warm up for a Heineken Cup match against Ulster by visiting the stand and showing off his fistwork.

It is unclear what precisely Patrick Bamford, the Ulster fan, said that so riled Brennan as he was stretching before coming on. Some suggested he called Brennan's mother an unprintable name; others claimed he made comments about Brennan's religion; still more said that Bamford had been disparaging about the Toulouse bar that Brennan owned. It was also alleged that beer was thrown at the player. Perhaps it was simply that Bamford was wearing a

Santa hat for a game in mid-January.

Either way, Brennan left the pitch and climbed up to the eighth row before his fists started flying. Bamford was soon needing treatment by the Ulster doctor for an inflamed cheek. He later said that he thought Brennan was coming to shake his hand. Toulouse said that their man had experienced "repeated provocation" and that "such supporters have no place in any sporting arena".

The event sparked great debate in Ireland and France. One caller to an Irish radio phone-in said that he recalled a junior game where Brennan was a spectator and ran on to the pitch to kick a player in the groin. He was certainly no stranger to violence. In fact, once the match against Ulster began he ended up brawling with Justin Harrison and got sin-binned. For the assault on Bamford he was fined £17,000 and banned from playing for life, although this was reduced to five years on appeal on the grounds that the injuries sustained by Bamford were not serious enough.

# 10  Springbok journalist disgusted by the Welsh

The tour to the United Kingdom in 1912-13 by South Africa, the second they had taken, was pretty successful on the field. They won all five internationals they played and lost only three of the 27 matches they played, to Swansea, Newport and a London XV.

It was the way they were received at other Welsh clubs that sparked an extraordinary article by the correspondent for the *Cape Times,* however. Clearly a sensitive soul, the journalist wrote that at Neath he "witnessed the foulest and dirtiest football I have ever seen and heard the most unsportsmanlike, bigoted, partisan and ignorant lot of spectators giving tongue, like a pack of yelping dogs, abusing in the vilest language the referee and our players". He said that he would be taking back "unpleasant recollections of Welsh manners" back to South Africa.

He was also disturbed by the crowd at Llanelli, whose "lack of control" encouraged the Welsh players to use "dirty tricks which mar the good reputation of rugby football". However, he said that the Llanelli fans were saints compared with those at Neath "who care nothing for the game or the way in which it should be played, provided that their own team wins". The matches were very close, with South Africa beating Llanelli 8-7 and Neath 8-3.

It is easy to pour scorn on the poor, sensitive Cape journalist. He may well have had a miserable time, although to a modern audience hearing about uncouth fans unsettling a sensitive South African is a bit like hearing the pot inform the kettle that he is black. Maybe some of those horrid Welsh manners were taken back to South Africa and, having been transplanted, grew into the fully formed rudeness that found its apotheosis in Mr Pieter Van Zyl?

# CHAPTER FOUR

## The Worst Off-field Incidents

# 1 Not so smart

There are several rugby players who have been given appropriate surnames. Paul Dodge, the dashing England centre of the 1980s, is one; Richard Sharp, the fly half in the 1960s, another; likewise Lewis Moody. Fran Cotton was always going to work in the textiles industry. But there are occasional contradictions, such as Neil Back, James Hook and, in the 1980s, Colin Smart, pictured on page 75.

Smart was a prop for Newport who earned 17 caps for England between 1979 and 1983. He was not selected for the England side that won the grand slam in 1980 but was a regular member of the side in 1982 when England began the Five Nations with a tricky trip to Edinburgh. It was a tough, defence-heavy game that ended 9-9 but only after a stupid tackle off the ball by Smart on Iain Paxton had given Scotland a penalty to level the game with barely any time left.

England lost to Ireland by one point, but went on to France and crushed the home side 27-15. Naturally some celebrating was in order and it was here that Maurice Colclough, the England lock, hit on a brilliant practical joke. At the banquet after the match each England player found a bottle of French aftershave next to their plate, a gift from the French RFU. Checking that no one was looking, Colclough emptied his bottle and filled it with white wine, then leapt to his feet and challenged anyone to follow his lead of downing the bottle of "aftershave".

Smart was up for the challenge – and a few minutes later was on his back in the back of a French ambulance on his way to hospital. Steve Smith, the England captain, said that "Colin may not have looked too much but he smelled lovely", while the man himself from his hospital bed admitted that it was "about par for a rugby dinner".

Smart was back in the team for the next match at Twickenham, where England beat Wales 17-7. "The after-shave will flow tonight," Smith said.

# 2 Carling sniffs at old farts

**N**o one stands on their dignity in the face of commonsense like the members of a British sports governing body. A sportsman can bring unheard-of success to the country but if he says one word out of line he can swiftly be cast adrift by the men in suits. So it proved for Will Carling in 1995. When Carling was made England's youngest ever captain at the age of 22, the team was in a feeble state. Within just over six years and in 48 games, he had led them to three grand slams (1991, 1992 and 1995) and the final of the 1991 World Cup.

Yet in early May 1995, barely weeks before the start of the next World Cup, Carling was sacked by the RFU. His crime? An unguarded remark to a TV documentary crew, sparked by a row over players wanting payment, that the RFU committee were

"57 old farts". The comments were naive for an accomplished media performer, but the RFU's reaction was shamefully over-the-top.

Carling was asked to telephone Dennis Easby, the president of the RFU, who told him that he was not fit to represent England as captain. The decision was struck up by the RFU committee over dinner at the East India Club and Easby had not even informed Jack Rowell, the England head coach, of his decision.

What Easby and the farts had not banked on was the outrage from Carling's team-mates and with the World Cup less than three weeks away they were in a position of power. Rob Andrew and Dean Richards, the two most likely successors, issued statements that they would not accept the captaincy and other players let their unhappiness be known. Two days after being sacked, Carling was allowed back in for the price of an apology. A month after that Rupert Murdoch signed a £340 million broadcasting deal with the southern hemisphere unions that effectively ended the days of amateurism. The farts were gasping their last.

# 3  Cash for questions

**Y**ou can hardly blame the RFU for being worried about player power and the demise of the amateur game (see previous entry). Four years before Will Carling was dismissed, his name had been at the centre of an unseemly row over whether players should get paid for giving post-match interviews.

It is hard now, more than a decade after rugby became a professional sport, to understand how traumatic the dying days of amateurism were to some people. Rugby had always been seen as a sport you played for the glory of it rather than the lucre. There was something romantic, almost classless, about England being represented by lawyers, surgeons and policemen. But as the southern hemisphere moved rapidly towards surreptitious payment of players, it became harder for the big names in the north to justify giving up their time free.

In 1991, during what would be England's first grand-slam campaign for 11 years, eyebrows were raised when Carling and the rest of the England team refused to hold a press conference after their 25-6 victory over Wales in Cardiff. It was later revealed that Instyle Promotions, the agency for the players that was run by Bob Willis, the former England cricket captain, and his brother, was asking the BBC for a fee of £5,000 for their players to talk to the broadcaster after matches.

But Carling angrily refuted the suggestion that the players were seeking money for their time and said that Instyle had acted without the players' permission. The press conference boycott was simply because the players had not felt like talking, in part because they were fed up with the media calling them up at their homes and offices away from games. He promised to reinstate the press conference for the next match. But his card was now marked. The RFU clearly started to worry about their successful young captain's amateur credentials.

# 4  Death is no excuse

**S**orry to do another story about myopic rugby administrators but there are a few of them about. This one is about how a strict interpretation of the rules and the refusal to bend them despite compassionate grounds led to England winning the World Cup. Sort of.

It was 1993 and Wade Dooley, the 6ft 8in Preston Grasshoppers lock known as the Blackpool Tower, was nearing the end of an illustrious career for England. One final challenge awaited: the Lions tour to New Zealand. But the tour had barely begun when his father died and Dooley flew back to Britain. His replacement was a 23-year-old Leicester lock called Martin Johnson who had only one England cap to his name. Things work out okay for Johnson in this story, however. It is

Dooley who was let down badly.

The New Zealand rugby union had kindly said that Dooley could return after the funeral if he wished, but Dooley initially told the England management that he was unlikely to do so. Put this down to the rash judgment of a grieving man, as a week later Dooley rang up the Secretary of the Four Home Unions, Bob Weighill, and said he had changed his mind and would like to return. Dooley had spoken to Geoff Cooke, the Lions manager, who had told him that he was needed back in New Zealand after a few shaky matches.

Weighill reported this back to the RFU, who were adamant that the tour squad should be limited to 30 players as originally agreed (even though their New Zealand counterparts said they had no problem with it being increased to 31). Dooley was told that he could travel but not be part of the squad, which he refused. Not only that, but Dooley decided that would be the point to retire from international rugby. It was a sad note on which to end. But on the flip side, it did mean that the man who ten years later would lift the World Cup could begin his career.

# 5   Academic pursuits

**T**eam spirit is everything in university sports, but occasionally the boundary between student athletes and elite athletes gets blurred and this can upset the unity. Oxford suffered this once in 1987 when the "True Blue" mutiny by five American international rowers threatened to capsize the Boat Race preparations and three years later a similar clash between home-grown and imported talent threatened to overwhelm the Varsity rugby match.

The row was primarily between Brian Smith, a 24-year-old scrum half who had played for Australia in the 1987 World Cup, and Mark Egan, a club player from Ireland, who had worked his way up the Oxford structure. When Smith arrived at Oxford, he was following in the footsteps of David Kirk, the New Zealand captain at the World Cup. Under their successive captaincies, other international players were signed and Smith brought in an Australian as coach. This was disliked by some more traditional students, especially when ten members of the 1989 Varsity Match side, captained by Smith, were foreign.

Egan became captain for the 1990 Varsity Match and chose to ban Smith and three other players for a term for arriving late for a game. He ruled that the star players could return only if they showed their dedication by playing in college games. "This dispute is about who has control," Egan said. "If you are a member of our club you devote all your energies to it."

The match, with the star players still missing, was naturally fraught for Egan, not least when there was a security alert hours before the match and 60 Metropolitan Police had to search the stadium, but his side pulled together in adversity, as the True Blue rowers had, and beat Cambridge 21-12. Both Egan and Smith went on to much more important things. Egan is now a senior official at the International Rugby Board and Smith is the coach trying to put some zip into the England backs.

# 6  Specialising is definitely not on

**W**atching old rugby internationals from the 1970s on ESPN Classic can be quite eye-opening, not least in the way that the scrum and lineout operated. It often appears that when a scrum was signalled the nearest eight big blokes grabbed each other and fell into the arms of the pack opposite. None of the crouch-pause-and-engage of modern times, when the scrum is like two battering rams heading for each other. It was simply a means of restarting play. Likewise the 1970s lineouts had little discipline but certainly no lifting. Two lines formed, the ball was thrown over them with little accuracy and it went to whichever player's frantic wafting was lucky enough to make contact.

It is worth watching matches from the past to remind us how lucky we are in the quality and skills that modern rugby players have. Yet four decades before the wafting, hugging, skill-free 1970s, the International Rugby Board was already worried that players were becoming... well... too good.

One of the most controversial edicts issued by the IRB was put out on September 1, 1932, when the board condemned "modern scrummaging methods" and called on referees, players and club officials to abolish "specialisation among forwards" so that the spirit of the game could be preserved. It seems that the IRB's view was that forwards should be little more than "bulk", an obstruction for people to run round. God protect us from ones that can handle, kick or run with the ball.

Perhaps the IRB was simply worried about the way that the game was being overrun by high scores. More than 100 points had been scored in that year's Home Nations Championship, but perhaps the international board should have been more worried about the disintegration to the world game by France being thrown out of the Five Nations that year because their clubs were too professional. But that would have been too easy for a governing body.

# Coloured prejudices

**T**he sad history of race relations in South Africa blighted sport in the second half of the 20th century. Rugby was slower than some sports to boycott South Africa in protest at apartheid, but when it came the Springboks were cast out for a dozen years. Even now, 14 years after South Africa won the first World Cup they were admitted to and despite a policy of positive discrimination that is at times misguided, there is still a certain unease in the relationship between Afrikaner and coloured players in the republic. But at least they are playing as a united team.

Apartheid is often attributed to the racist policies of the post-war National Party Government, but its roots came much earlier. One of the most contentious telegrams of the 20th century, up there with the one from Australia to Lord's in 1933 protesting at the unsportsmanlike conduct of Douglas Jardine's Bodyline-bowling England cricket team, came in 1921 from a correspondent with the Springboks team touring New Zealand.

The author, disgusted by seeing a game between the Springboks and Maori, wrote that it was "bad enough having to play a team officially designated New Zealand natives, but the spectacle of thousands of Europeans frantically cheering on a band of coloured men to defeat members of their own race was too much for the Springboks who were frankly disgusted". That is, disgusted at New Zealanders cheering a New Zealand team who happened to include native New Zealanders against a team of whites.

The publication of the telegram sparked an international uproar, but it caused a problem for New Zealand, who were effectively banned from taking Maori players with them to South Africa. The legendary George Nepia, who played 46 times for the All Blacks, was not taken on their 1928 tour to South Africa. It is a sad betrayal of great rugby players such as Nepia that it took the international community six decades after the hate-filled telegram before South Africa were finally taken to task for their racism.

# 8

# Ireland fall prey to foot-and-mouth

**R**ugby matches have been cancelled for a variety of reasons: frost, floodlight failure, war... but in 2001 several Six Nations matches were called off by the outbreak of foot-and-mouth disease in the UK. While not for one second wanting to equate the postponement of a few sports matches with the personal calamity for farmers of having 10 million sheep and cattle culled, the spread of the disease nonetheless ruined a fascinating tournament.

It had begun with high-scoring wins for Ireland and England over Italy and Wales. When Ireland beat France two weeks later, it started to look as if their fourth-round match against England would be a title decider. But two days after Ireland's win against France a discovery was made on an Essex farm that would throw the whole competition into jeopardy.

Within days, the disease had spread to Northumberland and the EU put a ban on the movement of stumbling livestock.

This included Irish rugby players and although England suggested that their matches be played at neutral venues, the discovery of foot-and-mouth cases in France stymied that idea. Three Ireland matches were postponed until the autumn as a result of the disease. In hindsight, it was probably not the ideal time for England to lodge a bid to host the 2007 World Cup.

If the delay jeopardised England's standing with other rugby nations, it proved fatal to Ireland's hopes of a first grand slam since 1948. They did thrash Wales in Cardiff in the second of the rearranged matches and recorded a fabulous 20-14 win over England in the third game, but by that stage it was England going for the grand slam. Ireland's hopes had been shattered a month earlier when they lost 32-10 in Edinburgh. Not counting a tortured 23-19 win over the Six Nations new boys, Italy, it was the only game Scotland won that year. If they had played Ireland when they were meant to, it is likely that momentum would have carried Ireland through. And all because of a few limping sheep.

# 9

# IRA deny Ireland grand slam

**T**he foot-and-mouth outbreak (see previous entry) was not the only time that Irish dreams of a grand slam were spoilt by outside agencies. The 1972 Five Nations became the first championship not to be completed after Scotland and Wales refused to travel to Dublin for their fixtures. They had received death threats, purportedly from the IRA, and so Ireland were left with only two matches, away to England and France, both of which they won.

Beating those two away was, of course, not as hard an ask in 1972 as beating Wales even on your own doorstep, so Ireland's slam was not guaranteed, but the Troubles prevented them from having the chance. The reticence of Wales and Scotland was understandable. Violence in Northern Ireland had escalated since 1969 and three years later there had been an attack on the British Embassy in Dublin. Almost 500 people would be killed in the Troubles in 1972. So, despite passionate entreaties from an Irish delegation to Edinburgh and Cardiff, the Welsh and Scots stayed firm. France showed a degree of solidarity with Ireland by playing a second fixture in Dublin as well as their one in Colombes. Again Ireland won, 24-14, adding to the sense of frustration that they had not been able to test their mettle against Wales.

Normal service was resumed in 1973, although no one wanted to draw much attention to the defeats that Ireland suffered away to Scotland and Wales. In any case, they were close defeats and proved nothing. What was reassuring

was that despite similar death threats to those made in 1972, England decided not to stay away from Dublin.

In fact, they walked out side by side with their Ireland counterparts and were well received by the crowd, who gave them a five-minute ovation. The Irish liked England even more when they had the manners to lose 18-9 and at the post-match dinner, John Pullin, the England captain, took the opportunity to have a dig at the refuseniks. "We may not be any good," he said. "But at least we turn up."

# 10

# Does anyone have a pump?

**R**ugby was introduced to the United States in the 1870s and for a while was quite popular. The US even won the gold medal for rugby at the 1920 and 1924 Olympic Games, although the latter was the last time the sport has been included in the Olympics. But its popularity almost immediately collapsed and for 50 years the US did not play international rugby. When they ended their exile, it was in a rather farcical situation but they almost pulled off one of the sport's biggest shocks.

In January 1976, Australia were in one of their low-ebb periods. They had beaten England twice on home soil the previous summer, but the autumn internationals featured heavy defeats to England and Wales and a narrow loss to Scotland. A 20-10 win over Ireland was small consolation, but at least Australia could contemplate a straight-forward morale-boosting win over the US, their first international fixture since 1924, in Los Angeles on the way home.

A curious crowd of 7,000 trotted down to Glover Field in the Anaheim suburb to see what the sport was all about. And no doubt they were quite bemused, not least because the match did not start on time as a result of a deflated ball. Whether the US team had provided only one ball is unknown, but an announcement was made over the public address system: "Does anyone have a pump we can borrow?" Another obstacle Australia discovered was that the pitch was neither long nor wide enough and had not been marked correctly.

But never mind, the principles were the same and once someone had discovered a pump the game could start. That was when Australia discovered that these naive Yanks actually could play, after a fashion. Certainly they could tackle as hard as anyone.

Australia reached half-time 13-6 ahead. The second half was similarly tight and the margin of victory, 24-12, reflected very well on the hosts. Tonga and Canada remain the biggest sides they have beaten since that game, although they have pushed some famous names close on occasion. It is assumed that a pump is now a standard item of kit.

# CHAPTER FIVE

# The Worst Injuries

# 1 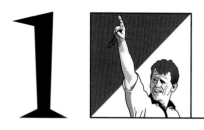 Wayne Shelford's ripped scrotum

**T**his will not be a happy chapter. Contained in the next few pages are tales that will make you wince, gasp and in some cases cry. Rugby is a rough game and sometimes people get hurt, sometimes very badly. While no one likes to see a player injured, none of us would want the physical element reduced.

That said, sometimes you have to laugh at the way that rugby players soldier on after the most hideous of injuries, especially when you look at footballers rolling around in agony after the slightest tap. One of the funniest injuries was that sustained by Wayne "Buck" Shelford, the New Zealand No 8, in what became known as the "Battle of Nantes".

Shelford was playing his second Test for the All Blacks and 20 minutes in he found himself at the bottom of a fiercely-contested ruck. As France piled in, scraping their studs over the prone New Zealanders, one of Shelford's testicles somehow got in the way of a boot. What happened next will make most men shudder. Shelford's scrotum was ripped open.

All Blacks are born tough, however, and instead of passing out, Shelford calmly told the team physio to stitch him up, which he did on the touchline before Shelford returned to the fray. "I was knocked out cold, lost a few teeth and had a few stitches down below," he said, rather understating the injury.

He felt that it would have been wrong to let his team-mates down by going to hospital. France were a tough side to beat then and six of the All Blacks squad were carrying injuries. He could not hobble away from the task. New Zealand still lost, 16-3, but Shelford's spirit made them tougher. A year later they won the first – and their only – World Cup.

# 2
## Callard's gashed forehead

**A** sure-fire way to guarantee a rough game with a South African state side is to beat the Springboks a few days earlier. Boks band together and when England did not just beat South Africa but smashed them 32-15 in Pretoria in 1994, Eastern Province were out for revenge. Or if not revenge then the chance to claim a few England scalps and give themselves the right to gloat at their capped countrymen.

England were superb in a no-holds-barred game where they took on South Africa up front and won. Brian Moore, Martin Bayfield and Tim Rodber waded into ruck after ruck, throwing aside men in green shirts, and creating space for Rob Andrew to score a crucial try. These were tough men, but Eastern Province thought they were tougher when the sides met in Port Elizabeth three days later.

That match ended in a 31–13 win for England but few remember the score. What they remember is Rodber becoming the second England player to be sent off after brawling with Simon Tremain, who was also dismissed. Rodber was an Army officer who should have known better, especially as he was captain for the day, although there were grounds for provocation. Tremain thumped him first – three times – and Rodber felt the need to ask him to stop in the bluntest fashion by punching back.

Naturally people got injured in such a rough game. For England, Graham Rowntree was concussed and Dean Ryan departed early on with a broken thumb. But the worst injury was that sustained by Jon Callard, the Bath full back, whose face was twice raked by the studs of the Eastern Province forwards. He left the pitch with blood pouring from his forehead and needed 25 stitches. Callard was unable to play in the second international four days later in Cape Town and South Africa squared the series with a 27-9 win.

# 3  Lend me your ears

**Sticking with dodgy South Africans (see previous entry), one of the big no-nos in rugby is sinking** your chops into an opponent. Yanking bits of them, scratching, kicking and kneeing are generally acceptable, but treating them as a piece of fillet steak is not. And it is not just rugby that disallows such things: remember Mike Tyson chomping on Evander Holyfield during a boxing match.

This feast in question was eaten by Johan Le Roux, the restaurant was Athletic Park in Wellington in 1994 and the food being presented for Le Roux's tasting was a juicy left ear belonging to Sean Fitzpatrick, the New Zealand hooker. Forwards often have cauliflower ears: Fitzpatrick's may as well have been covered in cheese, so tempting did it appear to Le Roux.

A bit of context: it was the second match of a three-Test series and South Africa's third match against New Zealand since being readmitted after the apartheid exile. Traditionally this was one of rugby's strongest rivalries and once New Zealand won the opening match in the series 22-14 in Dunedin, the Springboks were desperate to get back in the tour by fair means or foul.

Le Roux chose the foul route. He had waited 32 years for his Test debut, which came a month earlier against England, and was not going to waste time trying to make his mark. When Fitzpatrick drove him off a ruck, Le Roux turned round and nibbled at the Kiwi, who leapt away quickly, blood seeping from his ear. Le Roux was not sent off, but after seeing the TV footage South Africa sent him home in disgrace.

He was later banned for 18 months, which ended his career and meant he missed South Africa's World Cup win a year later. Not that he was repentant. "For an 18-month suspension, I probably should have torn it off," he said. "Then at least I could say, 'look, I've returned to South Africa with the guy's ear.'"

# More aural munching

**T**here is no logic in the punishments handed down to criminals. Johan Le Roux (see previous entry) was banned for 18 months for biting Sean Fitzpatrick's ear in 1994. Four years later the same offence only cost Kevin Yates six months – and unlike Le Roux it did not end his international career. It did, however, tarnish his name for good.

Perhaps the difference was that Le Roux's feasting was admitted and captured on television. Yates always protested his innocence and the incident was not clearly visible as it happened during a collapsed scrum. On the other hand, Fitzpatrick was not too badly hurt, whereas Simon Fenn, the London Scottish flanker, needed 25 stitches in his lug after Yates, the Bath prop, bit him. "I've never experienced anything like it," Ashley Rowden, the referee, said. "The player was clearly missing some part of his ear lobe. There was a lot of blood."

A three-man RFU disciplinary panel took four days deliberating what to do with Yates, who was asked to pay £23,000 costs as well as the ban. Some called for him to receive a two-year ban, although the lack of evidence probably saved him.

Yates had won his first two England caps against Argentina the previous summer and it could be argued that the ban, as it had for Le Roux, cost him a place at the World Cup. Clive Woodward, his coach at Bath who had been recently put in charge of England, said positive things about Yates being able to come back once he had served his ban, but it took him until 2007, a decade after his debut, before Yates was given two more caps, against South Africa. A spell in New Zealand with the Wellington Hurricanes helped his rehabilitation and after returning to play in England with Sale and Saracens he decided to end his playing days in French club rugby, where they serve more appetising meals than ear.

# 5  Little and large

**R**obbie Russell was brought up on a cattle farm in Australia, so he must have been used to dealing with big beasts, but he picked on one that was just that bit too big in 2002 during a club match between Saracens and Leicester. Russell, a diminutive hooker who had played a few Tests for Scotland without quite securing his place, almost ended his career prematurely with a reckless shove on Martin Johnson, a foot taller than him in height and a fathom bigger in stature.

It was a perfectly legitimate action. Johnson was shambling back towards a breakdown and Russell, who wanted to join the action rather faster than Jonno did, gave the big man a heave in the small of his back to hurry him along. Johnson was not happy. Over the course of his career Johnson had developed a reputation for thumping first and asking questions later. In 2000, the Leicester lock was cited by Saracens after punching Julian White and kneeing and stamping on Duncan McRae. He was banned for five weeks by the RFU. This time his response followed the usual pattern.

Turning round, he grabbed Russell by the collar, swung him back and punched him square in the face. Russell needed six stitches to a gash below his left eye. It cost him a place on the Scotland bench against Italy, although he did return and earn 20 more caps. He retired after a neck injury – presumably unconnected – and now earns a living selling ladies' footwear.

Johnson admitted his guilt. "I shouldn't have done it," he said. "I overreacted. I misread the situation." Yet he escaped with only a yellow card and ten minutes in the sin-bin. Saracens claimed later that he had been treated leniently because of his position as England captain. Leicester said that he had been punished enough and then, bizarrely, said that Johnson was regularly picked on by the media. The poor diddums.

# Max Brito

**W**e have enjoyed a good laugh at the expense of rugby players who have needed stitches after their team-mates bit them, but for some injured players it is no joking matter. Max Brito, in particular, leaps to mind. The dreadlocked Ivory Coast wing in the 1995 World Cup knew that he was never going to lift the Webb Ellis Cup. What he hadn't realised was that lifting anything would be an ordeal after the tournament.

Brito made his international debut as a replacement in the Ivory Coast's opening pool match, an 89–0 defeat against Scotland. He was an electrician by day, and the Ivory Coast felt that he could provide some extra power so started him against France in their next match, which they made a better fist of, losing by only 54–18. On the back of that, Brito was given a starting position in the Ivory Coast's third pool match, against Tonga.

The match was only three minutes old when Brito caught a high ball in his own 22, turned and ran towards the defence. He was tackled as he ran out of the 22 by Inoke Afeaki, the Tonga flanker. Several players bundled over the top of Brito, but when the umpire removed them all the wing was discovered prone and motionless at the bottom of the pile. Two of his vertebrae were shattered.

He was taken to intensive care in Pretoria, but while surgeons worked to repair his damaged neck vertebrae, Brito was left paralysed below the neck. He has been paralysed ever since. Brito and his wife separated and he now lives with his parents in Bordeaux. Worryingly, he has taken to talking about ending his life. "This bloody handicap," he said. "It's my curse and I will never accept it." Every rugby fan continues to wish Brito well.

# Matt Hampson

**L**ike Max Brito (see previous entry), Matt Hampson's rugby career was ended after suffering a serious neck injury. Where they differ is in the nature of the accident and their response to it. No one would for one second criticise Brito for giving up on life, but Hampson's positivity after his own critical accident is heartening.

Hampson is a fan of the film *The Shawshank Redemption* and has drawn inspiration from the film's message that "you get busy living or get busy dying". For Hampson, life changed dramatically on March 15, 2005, when the then 20-year-old prop was rendered a quadriplegic in a training session with the England under-21 side. He already had four caps for the age-group team and was clearly a talent in the making. England were preparing for a match against Scotland

and Hampson, a prop who had been with Leicester since he was in their under-16 age group side, eagerly took his usual position in the front row as the scrum went down. What precisely happened is unclear, but the scrum suddenly collapsed. Hampson was buried at the bottom, with his friends and team-mates piling in on top. Doctors later discovered that he had dislocated his neck and trapped the spinal cord.

It was a freak accident but one that rendered Hampson a quadriplegic. If Tony Spreadbury, the veteran referee and a paramedic in his day job, had not been there, Hampson may well have struggled to survive. Instead Spreadbury's prompt actions gave him the best chance of life but his rugby career was over in a flash.

It was an exceedingly hard thing to deal with. All those thoughts of things that you will never do again, not to mention having to rely on someone to feed and wash you. But since his injury, Hampson has put his energies into charity, both to raise funds for his own wellbeing and for general research into spinal injuries. He is believed to have raised more than £8 million.

# 8  Danny Hearn

**A**ll schoolboys who are mad-keen on rugby would say that they would give everything to play against the All Blacks. But do they really mean it? Danny Hearn was given the chance to test himself against New Zealand in 1967 and it ended up rendering him almost totally paralysed.

Hearn was a 26-year-old Bedford centre who had won a Blue for Oxford in the Varsity Match and was starting out in his international career for England, winning six caps in the 1966 and 1967 Five Nations Championships. He may well have represented England that autumn against New Zealand – they would lose 23-11 at Twickenham – so the match between a Midland, London and Home Counties team and the All Blacks was a good stage for Hearn to show what he was capable of.

Instead, all talk after the match was of whether Hearn would walk again, let alone ever run with a ball at Twickenham. His body was trapped in a heavy tackle that caused severe back injuries. Hearn was taken to the specialist spinal unit at Stoke Mandeville Hospital, where fears were raised that he might not survive, but not only did he pull through but he recovered sufficient movement to be able to coach rugby at Haileybury College for 15 years. In 1972 he published an autobiography, *Crash Tackle*. There might have been little appetite for it if he had been a mere England international.

Hearn also used his profile to speak out against the standard of some referees who were putting players' lives at risk. In 1996, he gave evidence in a £1 million lawsuit on behalf of Ben Smoldon, a 21-year-old hooker who was left quadriplegic when a scrum collapsed.

# Wilkinson's woes

It wouldn't be a chapter on injured players without mentioning the most famous ailing soldier of them all: Jonny Wilkinson. When that ball came towards him in extra time in the 2003 World Cup final, did he make a pact with the devil that if he could be given one wish there and then he would accept whatever ill fate was thrown at him?

That can be the only reason for the spate of horrid injuries that has afflicted him ever since that dropped goal. It began only two weeks after the World Cup when Wilkinson fractured a facet in his shoulder, which kept him out until after Christmas. That was just a trifling matter. He had barely come back for Newcastle when he had to go off again with a recurrence of the shoulder injury. In February 2004, he underwent the first of many operations.

By the summer, though, Wilkinson was right again and named as captain for the autumn internationals. He did not make it that far, however, because in October he was ruled out for six weeks with a haematoma in his right arm. It was not just his arms that suffered from the curse: early in January 2005 he suffered knee ligament damage during Newcastle's Heineken Cup defeat against Perpignan. On his comeback two months later, he damaged his knee again. Wilkinson's next recovery got him back in time for the Lions tour to New Zealand, but he suffered another shoulder injury in the second Test and missed the last one. That September, he was ruled out of the early season action after needing surgery on his appendix.

How he must be sick of anaesthetic. More surgery was to come in November 2005 for a groin injury and in May 2008 on his shoulder again, which kept him out of England's summer tour to New Zealand. In between he also had torn adductor muscles, more knee ligament damage, kidney damage and a twisted ankle that kept him out of England's opening World Cup match in 2007. And yet still he cheerfully says that he loves playing rugby.

# 10  Death on the field

**S**adly, sometimes injuries can be so serious that players are killed on the rugby pitch. This is extremely rare, with about 15 deaths in top-level rugby in the 20th century, but when they happen it shocks the sport. In 2008, Gareth Jones, a Neath scrum half, was hurt at a ruck during a Premier Division game against Cardiff. He was taken to intensive care with a neck injury and died two months later.

In 1996, 70,000 spectators at Twickenham for the Varsity Match stood in silence in memory of Ian Tucker, a South African-born centre who should have been playing that day for Oxford University but had died after being crushed in a tackle against Saracens six weeks earlier. The student was trying to stop a try, but his body became trapped under his opponent, crushing his internal organs. Doctors turned off his life-support system 24 hours after he was admitted to hospital. The previous high-profile rugby death was four years earlier when John Howe, a West Hartlepool lock, suffered a heart attack during a match.

Sometimes rugby deaths are simply bad luck. Other times, the death is caused by other players' wilful behaviour. Charles McIvor, capped seven times for Ireland before the First World War, died in 1913 after being kicked during a game at Trinity College, Dublin. More than 90 years later, murder charges were considered against a schoolboy in Canada after Manny Castillo, a 15-year-old forward, died of head injuries following a fight on the pitch. His family pleaded for clemency with his uncle saying: "They were not playing checkers. We truly believe it was a freak accident."

That was not the claim of the family of Riaan Loots, a South African fly half for Rawsonville, who was killed after receiving a stiff-arm tackle to the throat followed by a kick to the head by two members of the Delicious Rugby Club. The players were charged with Loots's murder.

# CHAPTER SIX

# The Worst Defeats

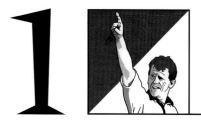

# Australia 76
# England 0.
# 1998

**F**orm in Europe counted for nothing in 1998 when Clive Woodward's England, triple crown champions a few months earlier, began what became known as the Tour from Hell. To be fair to the head coach, injuries and a series of unavailabilities meant that he was not able to put out his first-choice side for the opening international against Australia in Brisbane, but a 76-0 thrashing would have ended many other coaches' careers.

Australia, in fact, considered calling off the international after they saw the strength of the England team. Aussies like to wallop the Poms, but there is no fun in taking part in what would effectively be shooting fish in a barrel. The England XV, captained by Tony Diprose, had such little-known names as Spencer Brown, Scott Benton and Richard

Pool-Jones. And who on earth was this J Wilkinson, a 19-year-old making his first start at fly half?

The flood of tries did not become apparent at first. After 24 minutes, England trailed 3-0 and Tim Stimpson, the full back, had quashed two Australia attacks with ease. England could even have been ahead if Wilkinson had not muffed two kickable penalty chances. He would never amount to anything, people said. But then it began. Four tries were scored before half-time and another seven after the break as an all-star Australia threw off their shackles.

Stephen Larkham and Ben Tune each picked up a hat-trick of tries, with Tune completing his set in the final seconds that told you everything about England's day. Granted a penalty near the Australia line, England lost the ball on their own throw at the lineout and Tune scooped up the loose possession and sprinted 80 metres. The tour barely improved. England went on to New Zealand, where they lost 64-22 and 40-10, and then South Africa, where an 18-0 defeat completed the set. Oddly, England won their next international 110-0, but it was only the Netherlands they beat.

# 2  Scotland 0 South Africa 44. 1951

There is no shame in losing to South Africa, but Scotsmen must have been scratching their heads after a record defeat at Murrayfield in 1951. The Scots had been in decent, if not brilliant, form that year, beating Wales heavily in the Five Nations and losing to Ireland, the champions, by only one point. They also lost away matches to France and England by just two points. The margin was slightly greater when the Springboks came a-calling.

"Almost from the moment of the first try, there appeared between the two sides such a wide and ever growing disparity that the game developed merely into an exhibition," wrote EW Swanton in the *Daily Telegraph*. The spectators, according to Swanton, "seemed to revel in a detached unemotional way oddly out of keeping with an international occasion".

Scotland had perhaps been lulled into a false sense of security by South Africa losing two weeks earlier to a London Counties composite side. They should not have been; this was a strong Springboks side who had recently beaten the All Blacks away for the first time. Danie Craven, their coach and no bad player himself, regarded them as the best team he had seen.

The Murrayfield massacre was an immaculate display of 15-man rugby, with forwards and backs united to sweep wave after wave of attack at Scotland. The forwards scored seven of the nine tries and they were tries that forwards didn't usually score, running in from distance. "Feet, Scotland, feeeeeeet" went the usual cry from the home support as Scotland pressed forward for the first score, but play broke down and the 70,000 spectators were soon silenced. Salty Du Rand, the lock, scored the first try from a lineout and four more tries went in before the break.

More was to follow as South Africa battered Scotland at the scrum. Basie Van Wyk, the back row playing with a broken nose, finished the pick of the tries after 28 passes. It got so bad for Scotland that Angus Cameron, their captain, began to be given advice by his opposite number.

There is a story that after the match a depressed Scotsman was asked the score. "Forty-four nil – and we were lucky to get the nil," he said. Scotland did not win another international until 1955.

# 3  Penclawdd 4<br>Newport O.<br>1980

**T**here is a plaque on the wall of the Penclawdd clubhouse, which was presented to the Swansea-based side by Denis Thatcher, husband of the Prime Minister, that commemorates one of the great shocks in rugby. On November 15, 1980, Penclawdd, a journeyman side, downed the mighty Newport in the Welsh Cup. It was some way to mark the club's centenary – better even than receiving Max Boyce as the guest speaker at their celebration dinner.

Upsets happen, but this was in David and Goliath territory. Newport were one of the powerhouses of Welsh rugby, so respected that they were regularly given matches against international touring sides. A month before the Penclawdd embarrassment,

Newport had played with pride in a 14-3 defeat by New Zealand. Eleven years earlier, they had beaten South Africa. Penclawdd, known as The Donks, were still clinging to the glory days of the 1930s when they had provided both Wales half backs.

Haydn Tanner and Willie Davies were Penclawdd's national alumni, but the name of Kevin Dallimore can be counted alongside them after the open-side flanker's moment of heroism in the wet and windy fixture against Newport. With the wind – more like a gale – at their backs and the surface more of a bog than a pitch, Newport tried to play a running game that was better suited to a sunny day.

The turning point came when Keith James, the diminutive fly half who had played for Wales B, had his clearance kick charged down on his own line by Dallimore, who then had the presence of mind to fall on the ball and score what would be the game's only try. James's nickname at the time was "egg on legs". Egg on face would have been more appropriate.

# 4

# Cardiff 14
# St Peter's 16.
# 1993

**I**f Newport's drubbing in the rain by Penclawdd is not remembered as the worst upset in Welsh history then that is because 13 years later a bigger fish was toppled by a smaller one. Cardiff, mighty Cardiff, founder member of the Welsh Rugby Union, victors in their day over South Africa, New Zealand and – an astounding five times – Australia, were humbled at home by a fourth division side.

St Peter's RFC is now a feeder club for Cardiff Blues, but in the early 1990s it was a puppy looking up in awe at the beast down the road. Cardiff were the winners of the Welsh Cup five times in seven years in the 1980s; St Peter's sole piece of silverware was the Glamorgan County Silver Ball Trophy from 1984. Cardiff have produced more Wales players than any other club; St Peter's best player, Billy O'Neill, won his first Wales cap in 1904.

Expectations were so high that Cardiff's victory would be a formality, the home side rested half their first XV to save their strength for more testing games. Rumour was that extra space had been found on the Arms Park scoreboard for three figures, just in case. How often hubris is shot down.

St Peter's made their intentions clear early. Gareth Snook, their wing, ran in a try in the first half and with three penalties from Alun Edwards, the fly half, the minnows sent the giants packing 16-14. Rather churlishly, Alec Evans, the Cardiff coach, blamed the referee, calling him a "five-dollar official in a $20,000 competition". That his side won the Welsh Cup the next season was little comfort for the embarrassment.

Snook, appropriately for a wing, works for BAMC, an aeronautical engineering company and plays for the company side that has twice won the World Airline Rugby Tournament. In his spare time he is an amateur magician, as Cardiff can surely attest.

# 5

# Tonga 16
# Australia 11.
# 1973

**T**he Pacific Islands have had many rugby "upsets" over the years and bigger fish are constantly wary of these minnows in the World Cup, but 30 years ago they were barely granted matches by the leading powers, let alone holding hopes of beating them.

That changed, briefly, in 1973 when Tonga stunned Australia in their own Brisbane back yard. It was only their second proper international (excluding the annual games with Fiji and Samoa) and after being beaten 30-12 by Australia the previous week, there was little expectation that they could cause an upset. Certainly the home supporters had little interest; fewer than 10,000 turned up to watch.

If more had come, they would have witnessed two

tries from the men in gold but four from the Tongans. Isikeli Vave, the right wing, had the pick of them, finishing off a move by Kisione Mafi, the captain and No 8, who ran 40 yards from a ruck, while Tali Kavapalu clinched the winning try after a typical hard tackle from Valita Ma'ale turned the ball over. Ma'ale was something of a nutter, whose head-first approach to tackling gave him concussion in the first half. Fortunately for Tonga, he stayed on.

True, Australia in the early 1970s were not at their best. They lost series 3-0 to South Africa and New Zealand in 1971 and 1972, but those were almost written off as their opponents' wins rather than their defeats. It took the humiliation of losing to Tonga to make Australia realise that they needed to invest in developing young rugby talent. The world has seen the results of that investment in two World Cup finals.

Tonga, meanwhile, have not kicked on as some would have hoped. They beat France and Italy in 1999, the latter in the World Cup, but they have not enjoyed any more victories over either the southern hemisphere giants or the British Home Nations.

# 6

## Argentina 0
## England 51.
## 1990

**A**rgentina's defeat at Twickenham would be memorable enough for the scoreline, but the brainless act of violence near the end by Federico Méndez, the loose-head prop, has ensured that the game has lingered in infamy. With ten minutes remaining, Méndez, still a schoolboy, flattened Paul Ackford, England's lock, with a punch straight out of *Rocky.* Ackford went down, Méndez went off. He was later given a four-week ban. Méndez had only been summoned from Argentina because Luis Lonardi, another prop with a short fuse, had been sent off and suspended during their match against Ireland B.

The game was lost by the time Méndez saw red. England were 33-0 ahead and while the men in white were rather guilty of provocation, there was little cause for Méndez to react. Perhaps his head was woozy after having made a long run, taking the ball in the unaccustomed position of centre and making more ground than his backs had. But when play broke down, Jeff Probyn trampled on Méndez at the ruck and the Argentinian retaliated against the first white shirt he saw.

The match itself was a walk in the park for England, who were showing signs of the pedigree that would take them to a grand slam and a World Cup final the next season. Rory Underwood ran in three tries, Jeremy Guscott two and there were further scores for Jon Hall and Richard Hill. Simon Hodgkinson, given the luxury of no pressure, converted ten of his 11 kicks for a record haul of 23 points.

It should not have been that easy. Argentina were a developing side in 1990 but had already pulled off a few shocks. In fact, they had beaten England 15-13 in Buenos Aires that summer, with Hernan Vidou kicking five penalty goals to a try by Nigel Heslop and more points from Hodgkinson. These days, of course, ill discipline is more of an England curse.

# 7

Southland 19
Wairarapa 16.
1929

The Ranfurly Shield, known as the Log of Wood, is one of the most prestigious trophies a New Zealander can win. Initiated in 1904, it is played for on a challenge basis with the holders forfeiting it to any club that beats them.

Wairarapa, from the North Island, had won the shield for the first time in 1927 when they ended Hawke's Bay's record of 24 defences and although they lost it later that season to Manawhenua, they regained the shield by beating Canterbury and held on to it throughout the whole 1928 season. Although a faded force these days, Wairarapa in those days supplied 11 members of the New Zealand national side and they were expected to win their match against Southland, from Canterbury, with some ease.

So confident were they, in fact, that Wairarapa had not brought the Log of Wood with them to the game. It was on display in a shop window in Masterton, 20 miles away from the ground, and an embarrassed match official had to get in his car and drive to retrieve it after the final whistle.

Southland lost the shield to Wellington after their third defence and, after a couple of wins in the late 1930s, last held it in 1959. Wairarapa's relationship with the Log of Wood was even more short-lived. Victims of their arrogance in 1929, they won the Ranfurly Shield only once more, in 1950 against Canterbury, but lost it to South Canterbury in their very next match. They merged with Bush RFC in 1971 and as a result of playing at a low level rarely were given the chance to play a Ranfurly Shield-holder. In 2006, however, Wairarapa Bush were drawn against Canterbury in the cup and hopes were kindled that the shield would be coming home. They were soon dashed: Canterbury won 96-10.

# 8

## Wales 46
## United States 0.
## 1987

**P**erhaps you might think it odd to include this straightforward win for Wales in a chapter on unexpected defeats. Wales, after all, while not quite the force they were in the 1970s, were never expected to lose to the lowly United States. Where the controversy comes in this game, however, was in the decision to award full international caps to the players who trotted out an easy win against such a weak side.

The match will always be memorable for Bleddyn Bowen, the fly half, who scored two tries in his first match as captain, and Tony Clement, the 19-year-old Swansea full back, who came off the bench to score two tries himself. But purists felt a bit uncomfortable that this match was awarded the same status by the WRU as games against the All Blacks and England.

Not only had the USA not won an international rugby match against any opponent of note since beating France in the 1924 Olympic final, but they had not even put out their first XV against the Welsh. Eleven of the American side that played in that year's inaugural World Cup – and lost heavily to England and Australia after a narrow win against Japan – were missing.

The Wales team, by contrast, contained some greats of the day: Robert Jones, Paul Thorburn and Bob Norster. They had also come third in the World Cup that year. It was clearly a gross mismatch and should not have been called a full international. For Stuart Russell, however, a Kenya-born lock of little distinction, it was a special match. It would turn out to be his only game for Wales and thus his name is always linked in history with those of Gerald Davies, Gareth Edwards and Shane Williams.

# England 6
# South Africa 42.
# 2008

**E**ngland have had heavier defeats than the drubbing that they were given by the world champions but never at home. The most worrying thing, though, was that South Africa appeared to be playing within themselves. With a little more application, they could have put 50 points past Martin Johnson's side.

The previous heaviest defeat of England at Twickenham had been New Zealand's 41-20 win in 2006, which was the only previous time England had conceded more than 30 points on home soil. Johnson, England

coach for only two games, was quickly discovering that management was not as easy as captaining a side. His team won their first game of the autumn, against the Pacific Islands, but failed to put away chances against Australia and lost a match they could have won.

Defenders of Johnson and his team pointed to the relative inexperience of the side that he had selected. Paul Sackey was almost the grandfather of the team with only 20 caps. England were a team in transition and should not have expected to beat the Springboks. But 42 points at

Twickenham? It matched the 36-0 drubbing they had been given by the same side a year earlier in the World Cup.

The first half was a game of watch and wait for South Africa. The *Guardian*'s correspondent described them as being "like a schoolyard bully, almost holding England at arm's length". England thrashed away but could not make the breakthrough and South Africa got the first try from a close scrum. A second try followed after Danny Cipriani, acclaimed as the Messiah but acting like a very naughty boy, had an attempted clearance charged down. Ruan Pienaar gleefully gathered the ball and scored.

With half an hour to go, South Africa effectively had the match won. Only then did the shackles come off. Adi Jacobs and Bryan Habana took advantage of England's tired legs to run in tries from long distance, while Jaques Fourie was given the softest of tries after England panicked in defence. It was messy play, indicative of a team lacking leadership. Who would have thought that of any side run by Martin Johnson?

# 10

## Alcester 194
## Coventry Saracens 3.
## 2009

**I**t is never easy to compete with another side in rugby when you show up with only half a team. And it is especially hard when four of your eight players are lumbering front-row forwards, whose chasing and tackling is maybe not what it used to be.

So a heavy defeat was on the cards when Coventry Saracens arrived at Alcester in 2009 with only eight men, although the final margin was more like a cricket score. Coventry had a full front row and a reserve – although the latter was pressed into service when it became apparent that the team were a few men short – so scrums could be properly contested, even though Coventry barely had enough players to form a full pack. Sportingly, Alcester put only five men in the scrum themselves, against Coventry's three, to make it a bit more of an even contest, although that just gave the home side more options to use in the backs.

The Midlands Six West (South East) division match was slightly one-sided therefore. Alcester, who needed to win to keep their promotion hopes alive, ran in 32 tries and by the final whistle had passed the previous English record score of 177-3, set by Norwich against Eccles & Attleborough in 1996, and set a new benchmark of 194-3. Coventry's points came from a first-half dropped goal. It was a slight reverse on the match at Coventry earlier in the season, which Alcester won by a mere 29-3.

"Our game plan was to kick the ball far into their half and make sure they had to run the full length of the pitch," a Coventry player said. "With some handling errors, they helped to keep the scoreline lower than it could have been."

Alcester's tally fell well short of the world record score of 350-0 set by French club side Lavardac against Vergt in 1984. Frustratingly, the Alcester win was later declared void by the RFU because scrums needed a minimum of five players to be legitimate.

# CHAPTER SEVEN

# The Worst of England

# 1 The Andy Robinson era

Some people are natural leaders, while some are ideal sidekicks. And some are just unfortunate to be in charge during a recession and find that nothing you can do makes any difference. Andy Robinson may well have sympathy for Gordon Brown after finding himself in charge of the England rugby team at one of their lowest points in history. Was it Robinson's fault that England lost eight of their last nine matches in 2006? Not entirely. Was there much he could have done to change things? Possibly not.

Robinson, a former England flanker despite being only 5ft 5in tall, had a decent track record as coach of Bath – they won the Heineken Cup under him – and as the England forwards coach under Clive Woodward. He played a full part in ensuring that England won the 2003 World Cup, but his problems started when Woodward stepped down. It is never easy to follow a hero, especially when half the players who won the World Cup have retired or are injured.

England's first match under Robinson was against lowly Canada, rugby's equivalent of a bowler letting the batsman get off the mark with a long hop in cricket. England duly won 70-0. All good so far. It got better: they beat South Africa comfortably and although Australia had a two-point win to spoil a perfect autumn it was not a bad start.

A disastrous Six Nations followed in 2005. But in three successive matches, against Wales, France and Ireland, Robinson's team lost close games by less than one score. It started to look like they lacked bottle. A further narrow defeat followed that autumn against New Zealand, but Australia were beaten so again Robinson's report card read "promising, room for improvement".

2006 was an annus horribilis, however. A heavy win over Wales, the previous year's grand slam winners, was a false dawn and defeats followed against Ireland, France and Scotland. The predictable happened on the summer tour to Australia and New Zealand which meant that the pressure was on for the autumn internationals. Alas for Robinson, New Zealand put 41 points past his boys, then Argentina won only their third game against England and finally South Africa won one of their two matches. A tearful Robinson, defiantly saying that he had the support of the dressing room, was put out of his misery.

# 2  Back of the hand

**M**unster had more than their fair share of misery in the Heineken Cup before they won the first of two titles in 2006. Beaten by one point by Northampton in the 2000 final, it is the defeat to Leicester in 2002 that still rankles and Neil Back's "hand of God" that relieved the pressure on the English side near the end.

Leicester were leading 15-9 in the last minute, but Munster had a scrum in front of the posts and were looking for one last heave to change the game. Back, the flanker, saved it for Leicester in the most sensible, if despicably dirty, way possible. He cheated. With a furtive look to make sure that Joel Jutge, the referee, wasn't looking, Back stuck out a hand and swatted the ball from Peter Stringer's grasp as the

Munster scrum half went to feed the scrum. The ball came back on Leicester's side and it was cleared to safety shortly before the referee blew the final whistle.

Naturally, there was an uproar. Newspapers questioned whether Leicester's win was tarnished. "Are they really the best side in Europe or do they just cheat better than anyone else?" asked one, ignoring that there was no guarantee that Munster would have scored a try. To the credit of Munster, they did not create a fuss. In fact one of their officials privately admitted: "If one of our guys had done it, they'd have been made lord mayor."

Back, with the repentance of a cleared criminal, admitted afterwards that he wished he had kept his hands to himself. "I don't like people thinking I'm a cheat," he said. "It has tarnished my reputation. I would hope people will evaluate me over my whole career and not label me on that one moment. It happened spontaneously. As far as dirty play is concerned, I'm as clean as you can get."

# 3  Underwood underwhelms

**I**t is probably churlish and ungrateful to point out the blemishes on the record of such a fine player as Rory Underwood, RAF fighter pilot and England's own wing commander in some of their most memorable wins. But it is a tribute to Underwood's constant reliability that two glaring gaffes stand out in an otherwise impeccable career that featured 50 tries for England and the Lions.

Both came against Wales at the Cardiff Arms Park, which perhaps explains his lapse. The roar of 50,000 Welshmen exhorting their maker for you to slip up can break a man's spirit and when you are an England wing – and your forwards hold on to the ball for most of the game – it is easy to let your attention wander out on the touchline.

The first blooper was in 1989. England were leading 9-6 at half-time on a soggy day, but Wales hit them from the kick-off with a return kick down Underwood's throat, which he fumbled. Wales pushed forward from the scrum and again sent the ball spiralling Underwood's way. This time he held the catch but, perhaps in astonishment, stood there a while considering his options before throwing the ball without looking to Dewi Morris, who wasn't expecting it. Wales scored a try in the confusion and it proved the difference.

Four years later, Underwood had enhanced his reputation as a try-scoring genius only for Wales to unpick it. England led 9-3 this time and were looking good for the grand slam. This time a kick over his head was to prove Underwood's undoing. He trotted back too casually, looking over his inside shoulder to check there were no Welshmen following. Unfortunately, he didn't hear the thundering hooves of Ieuan Evans coming up on the outside to score a game-winning try. As they had four years earlier, Wales controlled the game once they were in front and England were left to blame Underwood for defeat.

# 4 Watch out for the post

Like Underwood (see previous entry), Hal Sever was a legend of his time. The wing made his debut for England in the famous win over New Zealand at Twickenham in 1936, scoring one of England's three tries (Prince Obolensky, the Russian émigré, getting the other two). He scored tries against Ireland and Scotland and dropped a goal against Wales in the 1937 Home Nations Championship. England won the three games by a combined total of five points, so Sever could certainly claim "National Hero" status.

The final match of a career curtailed by war came at home against Scotland in 1938. Again, the triple crown was at stake for the winner and Sever, who scored in England's season opener against Wales, was the star attraction. There was a second reason for him to want a good game: this was the first rugby match to be televised on the BBC.

England struggled in the first half and conceded four tries, although they were kept in touch at half-time by three penalty goals from Grahame Parker. A reinvigorated England resumed after the break, running into the wind, and won enough possession to clinch the game several times over. Yet the Scotland defence kept holding firm against wave after wave of attacks. Both sides could only score from kicks and Scotland led 18-16 with less than ten minutes remaining.

Then Peter Cranmer, the England centre, punted the ball downfield and Scotland found themselves turned in a flash by England's flying left wing. This was Sever's moment, the coronation of Prince Hal. Except that having cut in towards the posts, Sever appeared to collide with the upright, losing the ball. In the confusion, Scotland captured it and ran back for their own match-winning try.

That is the story, anyway. Sever always claimed to his dying day, at the age of 95, that he had not run into the post but had instead been caught by the Scotland defence who tackled him from behind, forcing him on to the woodwork. The end result was the same, but Sever insisted that it was strong defence, not his short-sightedness that lost the day. Ideally the BBC would have the footage for historians to study, but sadly it appears that the collision was not recorded. Maybe Sever just moved too fast for the cameraman?

# 5  Dooley wades in

**F**orwards like to thump first, think later. It is simply their way. Generally they do not attract too much censure for their rough and ready behaviour. It is only when a lack of discipline is seen to cost their team victory that the knives come out. So it was in 1987 for England and Wade Dooley, the Preston Grasshoppers lock, when his assault on Phil Davies set the tone for a brutal, ugly match that neither side emerged with credit from.

There were mitigating factors: the conditions were terrible with Arctic sleet coming down sideways. Such weather does little to improve a forward's mood, particularly when his backs are fumbling the hard-earned ball that he wins. Furthermore, both England and Wales were in rotten form that year and the match was effectively a wooden-spoon decider.

Again, that ensured that things would be ugly. People came expecting to see a rugby match and instead they got a brawl.

The match had barely begun when Dooley punched Davies, the Wales No 8, breaking his right cheekbone. He did well not to be sent off. At 6ft 9in it was hard to miss him, but somehow the referee didn't see Dooley's assault. Given that Dooley was a policeman in his day job, you would not want to be a felon on the Preston beat.

Dooley was not the only culprit. Kicking and punching went on without abatement in the first half, most of the action off the ball, and the final penalty count was 22-15 against England. Added to 12 penalties against Ireland that season and 16 against France, it made for a lot of ill discipline. The RFU insisted that four players, including Dooley, were dropped for the final match of the season. But Wales were also rough: Bob Norster broke Steve Sutton's nose with his elbow and they showed little interest in playing rugby. Stuart Evans scored the only try of the game and Wales won 19-12, but this will be remembered for being a punch-up rather than a match.

# Whitewashed by the Boks

**W**inning the World Cup once is hard enough, defending the title much harder. No one has ever won two in a row and the winners of the first three (New Zealand, Australia and South Africa) did not even reach the final four years later. True, Australia came within a Jonny Wilkinson dropped goal of getting back-to-back wins in 1999 and 2003, but they struggled in their group match against Ireland, winning by one point.

So history was against England in the 2007 World Cup, especially as they had been going through a poor patch. Brian Ashton had come in as head coach to replace Andy Robinson and brought with him a reputation for attacking, flowing rugby, but England still lacked something. They lost to Ireland, heavily, and Wales in that year's Six Nations and had an unconvincing opening win in the World Cup against the USA.

Next up was South Africa, who seized their chance to embarrass England gleefully. In some matches, it is almost more important not to concede points than it is to score them. South Africa may have put 36 points past England, but it was the nil against their opponents that told the story. South Africa tackled hard, yet kept their discipline, barely giving England a sniff.

Their game plan was simple: kick, chase, tackle, win ball, score. They led 20-0 at half-time through tries for JP Pietersen and with Percy Montgomery slotting over most kicking chances they stretched their lead after the break. Pietersen added a second try to seal the win. The only flaw in South Africa's game was that they missed with three dropped goal attempts.

It wasn't just the result that hurt England. Jason Robinson, their talismanic full back, limped off with a hamstring injury and many feared that his participation in the World Cup – possibly his whole career – was over. Of course, it all got better. England gave themselves a good talking-to, learnt to win ugly and reached the final, where they lost a close game to the Boks. But as World Cup defences go, this match was dire.

# The Battle of Hastings

**F**ortress Twickenham held solid for England in the 1986 Five Nations, although there was precious little beauty in the way they ground out a 21-18 opening win against Wales, Rob Andrew kicking all his side's points including a penalty from 60 yards. A win is a win, though, and if England had been able to show such control away from home they could have been title contenders.

Instead they suffered two heavy defeats in Murrayfield and Paris. France beat them 29-10, but had to accept second place behind Scotland, whose win over England was even more comprehensive, 33-6.

It was described as a second Battle of Hastings for England, with the same one-sided result for the Saxon men. Gavin Hastings had already impressed onlookers with 18 points on his debut for Scotland earlier in the season and he extended his national single-game record to 21 points against England with eight goals from eight attempts. The last of his three conversions was particularly pleasing for him because it had been scored by his younger brother, Scott.

The defeat shocked England, who had genuinely felt they had a chance. The gulf between the sides was immense, with Scotland much faster, stronger and more mobile than England. As often happens, as the match got away from them English tempers got frayed and ill discipline broke out. England trailed only 12-6 at half-time, but whatever Nigel Melville, the captain, said to them in the interval clearly did not work.

Proving the contrary nature of the sport, Scotland went on to play Ireland, who had not won so far, in the final match needing a win to be sure of the title. It was St Patrick's Day, which probably explains why Ireland's spirits were high. They ran Scotland to the wire, but the luck was not with them and the visiting side triumphed 10-9.

# 8

# A clobbering in Cardiff

The history of rugby between England and Wales is long and passionate. It is, as one RFU official once memorably said, based on trust and understanding. "They don't trust us and we don't understand them." From the first encounter at Blackheath in 1881, a victory by eight goals to nil by England, to Wales's grand slams in the early 21st century, competition has been hard fought and while dominance has switched back and forth, the overall reckoning is neck and neck at 53-53 after 118 matches.

England won the opening exchanges but by the end of the 19th century Wales had found their feet in the sport. They won ten matches between 1899 and 1909, losing none and drawing just the once, at Leicester in 1904. That 14-14 draw may have been seen by some England fans as a sign that the cycle was turning again, but 1905 was a grim year for the English, who were beaten 8-0 at home by Scotland and lost in Dublin and Cardiff.

The latter was a humbling 25-0 watched by 30,000 baying Welshmen. The home side scored seven tries – although oddly they could only convert two – while England were unable to get a name on the scoresheet. Frank Stout, the Gloucester flanker who was captaining England in his last season of international rugby before concentrating on his career as an orthodontist, must have been fretting at how easily Wales were sinking their teeth into his men.

Wales led 12-0 at half-time and motored away after the break for their heaviest defeat of England in 22 matches. While they have put more points past England since that day, it remains the biggest winning margin more than a century on – some going given the increase in the value of a try from three points to five over the intervening period. Wales went on to win the grand slam; England won the wooden spoon for the next three seasons.

# Biffed by Les Bleus

In some ways, 1972 was a marvellous year for England. It's just that they had to travel to the other side of the world to earn any success. On their tour of South Africa, England won six matches out of seven, drawing the other, and conceded only two tries. Their 18-9 Test win in Johannesburg, sealed by a try for Alan Morley and four penalty goals out of five attempts by Sam Doble, the new full back, gave England their first unbeaten tour of the Springboks' heartland for 81 years.

Enough of the fond reminiscing. 1972 was also a hideous year for England as they failed to win a game in the Five Nations. It was the first time since 1907 that they had lost every match and while the Twickenham games were close enough (a 16-12 defeat to Ireland and a 12-3 loss to Wales) they were walloped on the road. Scotland won 23-9 in Murrayfield but the defeat that really hurt was the 37-12 hammering they received from France.

It was France's final match at the

old Olympic Stadium in Colombes, built for the 1924 Paris Games, and no doubt they wanted to give the place a fine send-off before decanting themselves to the Parc des Princes. It was especially imperative that France did well because Les Bleus were in something of a rut at the time. Champions only two years earlier, they had lost their opening match of this season 14-9 at home to Ireland and would go on to be well beaten away by Wales and Scotland.

Hurrah for Les Rosbifs, then, for gallantly agreeing to be the whipping boys at Colombes' last hurrah. Two years earlier, England had lost 35-13 there in what was to that point their heaviest defeat by France. It did not take long for that record to fall. France moved 15-6 ahead at half-time and then stretched away after the break with tries for Pierre Biemouret, Bernard Duprat, Jean-Pierre Lux, Jean Sillieres and, finally, Walter Spanghero, the captain. It remains the biggest defeat France have given England.

# 10

# Flambeed by the Cook Islands

**T**here are defeats, there are hammerings and then there are losses that verge on the embarrassing. England's 21-17 defeat by the Cook Islands in the Wellington Sevens in 2008 was definitely one of the latter. Consider the demographics: the Cook Islands have a population of just under 20,000 on a series of islands just 91 miles square in area; England have a population of more than 50 million in which to find a decent sevens side. England have won World Cups and grand slams; the Cook Islands are regarded as the sixth best side in the Pacific. And Fiji, Samoa and Tonga are some way ahead.

An upset was clearly a racing certainty, then, when England arrived for the third in the annual IRB World Series of sevens events. England had come a disappointing fifth in the series the previous year and while they had only narrowly lost in the semi-finals of the Dubai Sevens, which preceded Wellington, they had drawn with Canada in Dubai and lost to Kenya in the subsequent George Sevens.

On to Wellington, then, for a sevens

tournament they had never won and a gentle opener against these Pacific Islanders. Watched by 34,000, an England side that included five players from Guinness Premiership clubs lost their way. Their 21-17 defeat by the Cook Islands was followed by a 15-7 loss to Wales and a 17-7 reverse against Fiji, meaning they finished last in their pool. They regained their composure on the second day, beating Canada in style and then outlasting France and Argentina, but it was only to win the consolation Bowl trophy.

Such embarrassments can cost a coach his job, but the RFU stuck with Ben Ryan and gradually he turned the season around. England reached the semi-finals of the Twickenham Sevens and the final in Murrayfield to end the year again in fifth place. By 2008-09 they had finally worked out this game and were in fine form going into the World Cup Sevens after reaching four of their past five finals. Despite nearly blowing it against lowly Tunisia, holding on for a 26-24 pool win, they reached the quarter-finals where they lost a thrilling match in extra time to another Pacific side, Samoa.

# CHAPTER EIGHT

# The Worst of Ireland

# 1 Sixty years of hurt

**J**ackie Kyle can rest easy. After 60 years of questions from fans about what it was like to win a grand slam, the former Ireland and Lions fly half can at last point to other, younger men in green and say "go ask them" after his countrymen finally won a second grand slam in 2009.

It was a curious anomaly before 2009 that Ireland, who on their day can play with no less flair and physicality than their opponents, had won the Five Nations Championship outright only ten times, the Six Nations never and had just the 1948 grand slam to mark an unbeaten season. That year, the title was decided in a 6-3 win over Wales in Belfast at which the Ireland forwards were dominant, driven ever onwards by Karl Mullen, the inspirational captain and hooker. The next year, they won the triple crown but were denied the grand slam after losing to France 16-9 at home. No matter, another clean sweep would be along soon.

But the closest they would come was in 1951, when Ireland were held 3-3 by Wales in Cardiff, with Cliff

Morgan, the future Wales and Lions captain, making his debut, and in 1985, their most recent title, when they won against England with a last-minute dropped goal from Michael Kiernan but drew an ill-tempered match with France at Lansdowne Road.

It would be almost 20 years before Ireland even won another triple crown. Some years they lost their only match to France (2004, 2006, 2007), while in 2001 they did the hard part, beating France 22-14, but three matches were delayed because of foot-and-mouth and they lost the rearranged one against Scotland 32-10. Few could deny that the generation of players Ireland possessed in the early 2000s was magnificent (Brian O'Driscoll, Ronan O'Gara and Paul O'Connell deserve their places in history) but somehow they just could not finish the job. As this book went to print, they were hunting yet another grand slam, but would 2009 be their year or would Kyle be wearily preparing for another round of questioning in 2010? Fortunately for Kyle, in his 84th year, the questions could end.

# 2

# The biggest anticlimax

The ideal scenario that the organisers of the Six Nations seek each year is for the two best teams to play each other in the final match with both undefeated and a grand slam at stake. It happened famously in the Five Nations in 1990, when England took their huge reputation to Murrayfield in quest of silverware and came away with nothing, but in 2003 Martin Johnson's England were on their awesome run of 22 wins in 23 matches on the way to the World Cup and no one was going to stand in their way, not even the Irish president.

Not that Ireland walked out of their dressing room with forlorn dejection. England had developed a habit of slipping up in the final match of a grand-slam journey and Ireland were confident they had the players to thwart England. Perhaps the moment before the anthems, when Johnson refused to line up his team where he had been told, forcing Mary McAleese, the president, to walk on the grass to shake their hands, should have told them it would not be their day.

Sometimes a close defeat can be more disappointing than a heavy one, but no one wanted to raise that point when Ireland lost 42-6. They trailed 13-6 at half-time after a try by Lawrence Dallaglio from a wheeled scrum and two Jonny Wilkinson dropped goal specials but were never really in the second half. England's rock-solid defence withstood anything thrown at it and Mike Tindall, Will Greenwood (twice) and Dan Luger had the firepower to pick up 29 unanswered points. "It's been a long time coming," Dallaglio said after England won their first grand slam for eight years. It had been rather longer for Ireland.

# 3  Namibia v Ireland

**B**eaten at rugby by a former German colony, how embarrassing. Rugby had been played in Namibia since the First World War, but the country formed its rugby football union only in 1990, which came too late for them to qualify for the World Cup the following year. They had honed their skills in the Currie Cup, however, coming third in 1989 in the South African domestic competition, and Ireland should have been more wary when they arrived in Windhoek for a summer series in 1991.

It had been a rotten year for the Irish, their only points in the Five Nations coming from a 21-21 draw with Wales, and perhaps they thought that a couple of internationals against one of the game's true minnows would buck their confidence before that autumn's World Cup. If so, they should have asked Wales, who won two close matches in Windhoek in 1990, or Italy, who lost twice there, about how easy it would be.

Namibia made the ideal start to the first match when Jaco Coetzee slotted over a dropped goal from 30 metres out. Andre Stoop, the full back who went on to play rugby league for Wigan, ran in a try to give Namibia a half-time lead of 9-0. Ireland got back in the game when they were awarded a penalty try by Clive Norling after Namibia's scrum collapsed, but Coetzee added two more penalty goals for a 15-9 win. A week later Ireland conceded five tries and let slip a 12-10 lead to be beaten 26-15.

Namibia qualified for the 1999, 2003 and 2007 World Cups but have yet to win a game. They did, however, give Ireland a scare in the latter tournament. The Irish were the fifth-best side in the world rankings but could not fire in that tournament. They conceded two tries in the second half, which Namibia won, but had fortunately got enough points in the bag before the break to avoid a third upset.

# 4

# Paddy O'Haka

**T**here is boldness and bravery in making it clear to your opponents before a big match that you will not be cowed, and then there is stupidity and senselessness in winding them up unnecessarily. Ireland strayed across the wrong side of the line in 1989 when they decided to square up to New Zealand at the haka.

True, the All Blacks can get ridiculously prissy about their war dance, objecting once to Wales's request to have a sing-song afterwards, but you need your brain examined if you decide to go nose to nose with a Kiwi when he is in his full tongue-lolling, eyeball-popping mood. This is what Willie Anderson, the Ireland captain and lock, did at Lansdowne Road. He and his team-mates linked arms on the halfway line and slowly edged forward as New Zealand performed until eventually Anderson was nose to nose with an inflamed Wayne Shelford.

"The Irish response was fantastic, it showed they were not going to back down," Warren Gatland, a member of New Zealand's squad that day and later the coach of Ireland and Wales, said, but what the *Daily Telegraph* called "this idiotic, discourteous whistling in the dark bordering on incitement" served only to whip up the visiting side.

The "Paddy O'Haka" as it became known was the preface for 80 minutes of lawlessness and rough play, with the lineout in particular becoming more about rubbing faces again than contesting the ball. New Zealand won 23-6 with tries for John Gallagher, Terry Wright and Shelford, who was happy to remind Anderson that when it came to getting in your opponent's face it mattered more if you could do it after the kick-off than before. It was the heaviest defeat Ireland had suffered against the All Blacks and while that was to change over the next 20 years, the memory of such a bold and foolish challenge has not dimmed.

# 5   Lost at the death

Is there any satisfaction in being a gallant loser? Is it possible to look back on a game that has been snatched from you in the final minutes and think "well at least we put up a good fight"? No, thought not. Over the years, Ireland developed a reputation for being a 60-minute team. Great up until the final quarter and then suddenly gaps would appear in their defence and better-organised teams would be through.

In 1934, it was worse than that. Ireland dominated Wales in Swansea for 70 minutes before conceding three tries in the last ten, which destroyed their hopes of a first win at the ground since 1888. Wales were generous after the game, as winners can and must afford to be, saying that Ireland had been the better team, but the fact is that for all their possession and passion, Ireland had not put any points on the board. Each time they attacked the line, they came up inches short. Their forwards kept winning the ball, but their inexperienced backs kept failing to use it. While Wales did score three tries in ten minutes, they needed only one.

However, it was Ireland who had looked like getting their name on the scoreboard first when with ten minutes remaining Aidan Bailey, the centre making his debut, intercepted a Wales pass and tore off for the line. Arthur Bassett, a fellow debutant, gave chase and hauled Bailey down with a crunching tackle in which Bailey lost the ball. Wales kicked downfield and Viv Jenkins scored – and converted – their first try.

Two more followed in the next five minutes. The appropriately named Albert Fear gave Ireland a jolt by wiggling over and then Cliff Jones, the fly half, swerved through the defence and sent Bun Cowey in at the corner. Jenkins converted from the touchline and Ireland were broken.

173

# 6

## Always the bridesmaids

**Younger readers from Ireland may wonder what all the fuss is about Munster always being** the bridesmaids and never the brides. The Irish province won the Heineken Cup in 2006 and 2008 and have a reputation for being one of the toughest teams to beat in the competition, especially at the Limerick stronghold of Thomond Park.

That is certainly true, but for much of the early days in the Heineken Cup Munster were known for being like the Ireland senior side, half of whom were Munstermen: great up until the final stages. Munster have a proud history, the only Irish side to have beaten the All Blacks, thanks to a 12-0 win in 1978, which they almost repeated 30 years later by leading 16-13 with four minutes remaining only for Joe Rokocoko to dash victory from their lips. But until they won the Heineken Cup for the first time, there was always a sense that they had not quite lived up to their reputation in the European competition.

Beaten in the quarter-finals in 1999, they reached their first final in 2000 with a memorable 31-25 win over Toulouse in the semi-final. That out of the way, Northampton should have been much easier but the sides met on a grey, rainy day at Twickenham and, oddly for a side with such strong forwards, Munster came off second best. Tim Rodber stole two Munster throws at the lineout and although Munster scored the only try, Paul Grayson's kicking gave Northampton a 9-8 victory. Ronan O'Gara had a penalty in the last minute to win the title, but his kick clipped the post.

Two years later, Munster were again in the final, but lost to Leicester after a flagrant bit of cheating by Neil Back near the end of the game (see chapter 7). In 2003, Munster qualified for the knockout stages by beating Gloucester 33-6 when only a 27-point margin would have sufficed but they lost in the semi-finals to Toulouse by one point. More heartache was to come in the semi-finals in 2004 when they led by ten points in the second half but lost after London Wasps scored two tries in injury time. It was getting agonising, but fortunately for their fans, Munster's luck was about to change.

# 7  All downhill from here

**I**reland's tour to Australia in 1994, only their second visit Down Under, came in the middle of the inglorious years between 1988 and 1999 when their best finish in the Five Nations was fourth, so few hopes were really placed on a talented but unfulfilled team coming back with a series win over the world champions, even if their meeting in the 1991 World Cup had been settled in Australia's favour only by a slender one-point margin.

However, there were some very happy memories of Ireland's previous tour to Australia, in 1979, when Ollie Campbell's accurate kicking ensured a 2-0 series win against their hosts and gave Mike Gibson, the legendary Ireland and Lions centre, a fitting final hurrah before retirement. Ireland had begun that series with a 39-3 defeat by Western Australia and went on to lose all five state matches before winning the Tests 27-12 and 9-3, which suggests that you should read little into warm-up games. Ireland should have realised 15 years later that the same can work in reverse.

They did not just win the first match of their tour in Perth, they annihilated Western Australia 64-8. It was a massacre. And maybe that started to raise hopes in the Ireland camp. Always dangerous.

The rest of the tour disintegrated: New South Wales beat Ireland 55-9, Australian Capital Territory won 22-9, Queensland nipped a 29-6 win and then an Australian XV won 57-9 at Mount Isa.

Ireland did claim a second victory of the tour, edging out a New South Wales Country XV on June 8, but that came in between two heavy defeats in the internationals. Australia won the first 33-13 and the second 32-18 to send Ireland home with their tails between their legs. That would teach them to get carried away.

# 8

# Georgia on their mind

**T**he 2007 World Cup will not go down as a happy tournament for Irishmen. Drawn in the same pool as France, the hosts, and Argentina, who provided several shocks that year, it was going to be tough just getting out of the group and Ireland duly failed to achieve this with a 30-15 loss to Argentina and a 25-3 beating by France.

Their other matches should have been more straightforward but, as you can read earlier in this chapter, Namibia provided a few worries and Georgia, playing in their second World Cup, almost provided a huge upset. Georgia are a developing side, whose strength is mainly in their forwards. French communists had brought the game to the Soviet republic and many of the players compete in France.

They should not have been much of a match for Ireland, however, which made it a shock to see that the final five minutes of their pool match in Bordeaux featured Georgia camped on the Ireland line, pushing for the try that would give them victory. Ireland had scored first in the 16th minute through a try by Rory Best, the Ulster hooker, but Giorgi Shkinin, the right wing, led a frantic charge into the Ireland half that resulted in David Wallace being sent to the sin-bin for killing the ball and a Georgia penalty, kicked over by Merab Kvirikashvili.

Then, five minutes into the second half, Shkinin intercepted a looping pass from Peter Stringer to Brian O'Driscoll and galloped away for a try that gave Georgia the lead. Girvan Dempsey put Ireland back in front ten minutes later but the game headed for a nervous finish. Georgia threw everything they had at Ireland and were denied a try by Denis Leamy, the TV official ruling that he had held the ball up. When the final whistle came, Ireland were very very relieved.

179

# 9   The Lansdowne Road caning

**H**istorically, it would be wrong to call Lansdowne Road a fortress – Ireland have been too inconsistent to build up many consecutive wins there, although they did win 18 of their 19 matches at home between 2002 and 2004 and were on a winning streak of seven games at Lansdowne Road when the stadium was knocked down in 2006. Whether they can continue the winning run when the new Lansdowne Road, unglamorously to be called the Aviva Stadium, reopens in 2010 remains to be seen, but it won't feel as homely and heartening. Or smell as faintly of stale urine as the old ground did.

In 1996-97, Lansdowne Road definitely was not a fortress. More a collapsed tent as Ireland lost six home matches in a row, the worst of them being a 63-15 humbling by New Zealand. All teams feel confident that they can put on a good show at home, regardless of the opposition, but the New Zealand tourists that year were on one of their awesome winning streaks and when they came to Ireland they had won eight matches on the trot, an unbeaten run that would be extended to 13 plus a draw before they lost to Australia in 1998. A tough ask for Ireland.

It was made tougher by the selection of seven debutants in green jerseys. Talk about lambs to the slaughter. Many of the new boys would go on to achieve little, their confidence shattered by a walloping in their first game, although two notable alumni of that game, Malcolm O'Kelly and Kevin Maggs, went on to become regular players.

Up against them were some of the most fearsome backs ever assembled: Christian Cullen, Jeff Wilson, Frank Bunce, Andrew Mehrtens, Justin Marshall... The only plus for Ireland was that Jonah Lomu, suffering from a kidney complaint, was not there.

Ireland actually competed for the first half, scoring 15 points with two tries for Keith Wood, but they would not score any after the break and New Zealand ran in seven tries in the game to get their northern hemisphere tour off to a flying start and silence the fans in Lansdowne.

# 10

## From triumph to despair

**I**reland won the 1974 Five Nations Championship without playing on the final weekend. Willie John McBride, who set a world record for appearances of 56 when he led Ireland to a 26-21 win over England (equalling Ireland's record score in internationals), was able to claim bragging rights at the end of the tournament when England beat Wales in their final match, meaning that Ireland, who had a week off and had begun their season with a 9-6 defeat by France, were the champions by virtue of beating England and Scotland and drawing with the Welsh.

It helped McBride's side that the referee at Twickenham, John West, ruled that JJ Williams's "try" for Wales near the end of the game had not been properly grounded. TV replays were inconclusive and it was surely only a coincidence that West was Irish. Even so, he ensured himself pints of Guinness for life after his intervention. It was Ireland's first title for 23 years and McBride and such team-mates as Mike Gibson and Fergus Slattery would form the bedrock of the Lions side that would win in South Africa later that summer for the first time in 78 years.

A great time to be Irish, then, which makes their collapse the next season so disappointing. Ireland beat England and France at Lansdowne Road, with McBride finally scoring his first international try in the latter after 62 caps, but a fortnight after the France victory Ireland's hopes were destroyed by a rampant Wales, keen to get revenge for having the title snatched from them the previous year. The 32-4 victory was the heaviest defeat Ireland had

suffered to one of the home nations for 68 years.

The Cardiff crowd were delirious with the win, which gave them the championship. Each of their Lions played his part: Gareth Edwards splitting the defence with frequency, Gerald Davies scoring the second try at speed and JPR Williams seemingly everywhere all the time. There was nothing that McBride, playing his last match, could do but shake his head and shake the Welshmen's hands. It was ten more years before Ireland next won in Wales.

# CHAPTER NINE

# The Worst of Scotland

# 1 Scotland v Italy, 2007

Every run of bad results has to come to an end at some point and after seven years in the Six Nations Championship without a win away from home, Italy's best chance of breaking that duck was always going to be at Murrayfield against a weak Scotland. What no one predicted was how straightforward and one-sided the game would be.

The game was won and lost in the first six minutes when Scotland were surprisingly generous to their guests, not just giving away three tries but wrapping them up in glitzy paper, tying a ribbon round them and writing Italy a card in beautiful calligraphy. Phil Godman got the party going after just 18 seconds when he received the ball inside his own 22 and tried a cunning chip over the upcoming Italy defence rather than the usual huge hoof. Mauro Bergamasco charged the ball down and gathered it to score. 7-0 to Italy and 79 minutes to go.

Then Chris Cusiter took over the self-destruct button, first popping up a pass to Rob Dewey that was intercepted for a try by Andrea Scanavacca and then giving the same treat to Kaine Robertson with an ambitious long pass to Hugo Southwell that was so telegraphed that it had a franking mark on it. 21-0 to Italy with 74 minutes to go.

That was more or less game over before some spectators had settled into their seats. Scotland needed to strike back quickly and Dewey got the home side on the scoreboard on 13 minutes but then they lost Simon Taylor to the sin-bin, which only made the task harder. The sides exchanged penalties, giving Italy a 24-10 half-time lead. Chris Paterson pulled the hosts back within seven points and with 20 minutes to go there was still hope for Scotland, but Alessandro Troncon burrowed over for Italy's fourth try and Scanavacca kicked penalties to give Italy a 37-17 win.

# 2

## Trophy abuse

**T**he Calcutta Cup is one of the most distinctive trophies in sport. Eighteen inches high, with handles that resemble king cobras and an elephant on the lid, it was fashioned from melted silver rupees that belonged to the Calcutta Rugby Club and was donated to the RFU in 1877 to be competed for annually. Originally the plan was for it to be rugby's version of the FA Cup, but competition between clubs ran contrary to the RFU's amateur ethos and so it was instead used for the annual match between Scotland and England.

Like the Ashes urn, the original Calcutta Cup is now too fragile to be presented to the winning teams – they use replicas instead – and its fragility cannot have been helped by the treatment given to it by John Jeffrey and Dean Richards, the Scotland and

England back-row forwards, after the match at Murrayfield in 1988.

As with all the best rugby stories, this begins with lots of alcohol. England had won their Five Nations match 9-6 and by the time they arrived for the post-match dinner Scotland had already begun to drown their sorrows. A childish food fight broke out and soon escalated, although the committee men of both unions who were pelted by stray bread rolls may not have been as amused as the players.

Tradition at the time allowed for the holders of the Calcutta Cup to drink from it, so England topped it up with champagne and passed it round, occasionally emptying the contents over their team-mates. Then Jeffrey, a farmer, and Richards, a policeman, thought it would be a good idea to take the trophy for a walk. Well, more of a rolling maul than a walk. The cup, valued at £10,000, was heavily damaged.

Richards was given a one-match ban for his role in using the cup as a ball but Jeffrey was much more sternly treated. He was handed a six-month ban and dropped from their international sevens squad. Professing a hazy memory, Jeffrey said: "I was absolutely blootered,".

# 3  Japan v Scotland. 1989

**S**cotland have played three full internationals against Japan, winning them 47-9, 32-11 and 100-8, so it is probably as well for the record books and the blushes of some international players that caps were not awarded for the match at the Chichibunomiya Stadium in Tokyo in 1989. Japan won 28-24, putting five tries past their guests for their first win against a top-tier nation.

True, it was a weakened Scotland team that had been presented. Nine of their first-choice players, including the Hastings brothers, David Sole and

Craig Chalmers, were on tour with the Lions in Australia. But there were 11 capped players in the side who took the field and Richie Dixon, the Scotland coach, said after the match that his team should have been experienced enough to handle both their opponents and the extreme humidity.

The Cherry Blossoms, as Japan are known, had been introduced to rugby by British sailors in Yokohama in 1874 and played their first international in 1932, beating Canada 9-8. They gave Wales a scare in 1983 before losing 29-24, so Scotland should have been more wary six years later. The Japan XV included the highly experienced Toshiuki Hayashi, named as a member of Oxford University's all-time best XV, and the speedy Yoshihito Yoshida on the wing.

Japan had been cunning in not allowing any of their international squad to play in Scotland's four tour matches, so the touring side did not have an inkling of the skill and pace that they would meet, especially from the centres Eiji Kutsuki and Seiji Hirao. Scotland could still have won the game handsomely if Cameron Glasgow, the full back, had shown the kicking form of his previous two matches, in which he landed 25 out of 30 attempted kicks. Japan were tremendously generous, giving away 23 penalties, many for killing the ball at the ruck, but Scotland missed seven kicks.

It would be unfair to blame Glasgow totally for the defeat, though. Scotland were sloppy and outplayed by a flamboyant Japan team, most of whom were in the side who won their first World Cup match, against Zimbabwe, in 1991. Scotland, of course, were grand-slam champions within a year.

# 4  Romania v Scotland

One of the disappointments in European rugby is that Romania could not turn their promising results in the 1980s into something more permanent. There was a time when it appeared that the Oaks, as they are known, could become the sixth member of an expanded Five Nations Championship after a string of impressive results against more fancied opposition. In 1981, they lost 14-6 to New Zealand but had two tries disallowed and they have had victories over Wales and France, but it was their win against Scotland in Bucharest that stands out.

Scotland were convincing grand slam champions in 1984 with big wins over England (18-6), France (21-12), Wales (15-9) and Ireland (32-9 at Lansdowne Road) and if they treated a summer trip to Bucharest with complacency, it was not reflected in a strong squad selection that included Lions such as Jim Renwick, Roy Laidlaw and John Beattie as well as other experienced players.

Perhaps it was the intense heat that got to Scotland. They led 19-12, but wilted in the second half, conceding tries to Mercea Paraschiv, the experienced scrum half, and Alexandru Radulescu, the No 8, for a 28-22 defeat. Champions of Europe in February, Scotland were second best in Eastern Europe three months later.

Rugby was introduced to Romania by students who had picked up the game in Paris. They won the bronze medal at the 1924 Olympic Games – although only three teams entered and they lost 59-3 to France and 39-0 to the United States – and the sport flourished under communism, with victories over the "soft West" being the target of a well-paid and disciplined training regime. As communism declined, rugby became unfunded and reduced to a minor sport but there was one last hurrah in 1991 when they beat Scotland, many of whom had won the grand slam the previous year, for a second time in Bucharest 18-12.

Peter Dods, the full back, played in both defeats, ignominious bookends to an otherwise successful career. Tragically, Florica Murariu, a flanker in the 1984 win who went on to captain the side, could not play in both wins. He was shot dead at a roadblock during the revolution in 1989.

# 5   Hancock's half-minute

**A**ndy Hancock only played three internationals for England but it is for the second of these at Twickenham in 1965 that his name will be cursed along the length of Princes Street, Edinburgh for decades to come. It has gone down in history as one of the great length-of-the-field tries, up there with Gareth Edwards's for the Barbarians in 1973 and Philippe Saint-Andre's at Twickenham in 1991, but while both of those were scored early in their match, Hancock left his effort until the final minute.

In fact, it was even later. Eighty minutes had passed and the referee was about to bring his whistle to his lips when Hancock began to gallop down the left wing. Scotland were leading 3-0 through a dropped goal by David Chisholm in what was a typically grim Calcutta Cup match. They needed to win to avoid the wooden spoon in that year's Five Nations and they had not won at Twickenham for 27 years. The longer the game went on the more desperate were England's attempts to create something.

As injury time began, Scotland had a scrum three yards from the England line, but the men in white won it against the head and Mike Weston, the fly half, kicked the ball for touch. He miscued it into the arms of David Whyte, who ran the ball back only to lose it in a tackle. Weston gathered and swiftly threw a pass to Hancock on the left wing. The Northampton wing, seeing only forwards in front of him, put his head down and ran full pelt. Ian Laughland, chasing from behind, dived to tap-tackle his heel, but though Hancock faltered he did not fail. Stewart Wilson, the full back, came across to intercept him but Hancock cast a gaze inside, which made Wilson hesitate, and then took off on the outside again.

Some Scots claim that he put a foot in touch as he ran wide, but the footage is inconclusive. What is certain is that Hancock was so exhausted that he collapsed in the corner, rather than running round behind the posts. It gave Don Rutherford a tricky conversion, which he missed, meaning the game was drawn, tries being worth three points in those days, but perhaps for England to snatch a win would have been far too cruel on Scotland.

# Not you again

There are some opponents who a side would be very happy never to play ever again after a crippling loss. In Scotland's case, it is New Zealand who they would rather avoid in future World Cups having played them in four of the six tournaments so far and been walloped each time. Three of those losses came in quarter-finals, leading some Scots to make the conspiracy theory that those who schedule the global competition have it in for Scotland.

Scotland have never beaten the All Blacks. As of 2009, they have played them 27 times and lost 25 but the fact that they had earned a 25-25 draw in 1983, to go with a 0-0 boreathon in 1964, gave a faint hope that they might progress to the semi-finals of the first World Cup in 1987. Five members of the team that had drawn in Edinburgh were still there four years later, with Peter Dods, another 1983 veteran, on the bench, so there were plenty of positive thoughts. Unfortunately, this time New Zealand were at home and they had not yet learnt to choke in World Cups.

The All Blacks scored only two

tries, for John Gallagher and Gary Whetton, but Grant Fox kicked six penalties and Scotland were broken, 30-3. The fixture list kept them apart in 1991, when Scotland reached the semi-finals, but in 1995 and 1999 their old friends were waiting for them in the last eight. The former they lost 48-30, the saving grace being that they stopped Jonah Lomu from scoring more than one try, while four years later they were beaten 30-18, although the winning margin rather flattered Scotland who trailed 25-3 at half-time.

To their relief they were not scheduled to meet New Zealand until the semi-finals in 2003, although Scotland decided to lose in the quarter-finals to Australia just to make sure, but in 2007 they were drawn in the same pool as the All Blacks. This time, to save morale and prevent broken bones, Scotland put out a second XV, deciding to rest their best players for the final pool match with Italy. In effect they had decided that the game was already lost and so there was no point trying to win it. Naturally, they lost 40-0. It says something about Scotland's mentality at the time that this was presented as a triumph.

# 7  A whitewash at home

**T**he Scotland faithful have seen many disappointments at home over the years, but nothing surely is more dispiriting than to see your team fail to score a point in two consecutive matches. This was their team's fate in the 1921 Five Nations when they followed a 3-0 defeat to France, Olympic champions the previous year, with a record 18-0 loss to the hated English.

The victory gave England the triple crown and, with a 10-6 win over France ten days later, set them up for a grand slam, which must have made the frustration for the crowd at Inverleith, Scotland's former home, more palpable. England's win was based on their forwards, who were quick and powerful in the loose, and while it took almost 20 minutes for the deadlock to be broken, once Reg Edwards crossed the line for the visiting side Scotland were never in the match.

Tom Woods, who like Edwards and another forward team-mate, Ernest Gardner, was actually born in Wales, scored England's second try from a lineout before the break to give England an 8-0 half-time lead, which was extended by second-half tries from Bruno Brown and Quentin King, who ran in from the halfway line. The latter was playing in his first and only Test, yet like Andy Hancock (earlier in this chapter) he remains a hate figure in Scotland.

This was a strong England side, but the scale of defeat and particularly the fact they could not score rankled with Scotland. Four years later they moved to a new ground at Murrayfield, which they celebrated by having a grand-slam season that included a 14-11 win over the Auld Enemy. They went on to win the championship in the next two seasons as well, with a 21-13 win over England at Murrayfield in 1927, perhaps proving that a change can be as good as a rest.

# 8 Gone in 360 seconds

**I**s it possible to be knocked out of a World Cup within the space of six minutes in your opening match? It is if you are playing in a sevens World Cup, where matches are seven minutes each way, and if you tackle as badly as Scotland did against Canada in Dubai in 2009.

It should have been a mismatch, but not in the direction that it panned out. Scotland were hardly one of the favourites for the tournament, but they had made the quarter-finals in six out of the eight IRB World Series events in the previous year, compared with Canada whose best finish was to come twelfth. With only the two best runners-up from the six pools in Dubai qualifying for the quarter-finals, Scotland needed to make a fast start against Canada to beef up their points difference and hope that they only lost narrowly to South Africa. They did the second part but not the first.

Within six minutes of the match against Canada, Scotland trailed 33-0 having given up five tries. The middle three of them came straight from the restart, with Canada grasping the ball first and tearing through a rather static defence for the easiest of scores. Scotland scored two tries through their captain, Colin Gregor, in the second half but it was too little too late and by virtue of having been hammered Scotland's World Cup was over.

The frustrating thing is that once the first half of the tournament was out of the way, Scotland played quite well and with the winners being Wales, the 80-1 outsiders before the event, there were some gnashing teeth and ruminations about what could have been in the Scotland dressing room. They went on to beat Japan comfortably and were hanging on 14-14 with South Africa before the Springboks scored in injury time. Scotland went into the second-tier Plate competition, which they won after beating France and Australia.

# Don't mention the fifties

To go through one season without a win could be a misfortune. Two seasons looks like carelessness. And if you do it for three seasons, well you just have to accept that you are hopeless. Scotland were particularly hopeless in the 1950s, with 11 wins, two draws and 30 defeats, including a string of 17 straight losses between 1951 and 1955. The only area in which they could say they led the way in that decade was in being the first team to install under-soil heating at their home stadium, which Scotland did at Murrayfield in 1959.

And to think that it all looked so rosy immediately after the war when Scotland won at Murrayfield against England, Ireland, Wales and a touring side of Kiwis (not representing New Zealand) and beat Wales in Cardiff in 1946. The win over the Kiwis was particularly impressive as it was one of only two defeats they suffered in their 27-match tour.

How quickly it all changed. Scotland failed to win a match in the 1947 Five Nations, beaten 24-5 by England at

Twickenham, and once the 1950s got going they soon settled into a losing rut. Victory over Wales, the previous year's grand slam champions, by 19-0 in February 1951, was surely a freak result. They lost to Ireland, France and England by narrow margins and then to South Africa by a huge, 44-point, barrier that is described in another chapter.

The next three years were even worse. Scotland failed to win a game in the Five Nations in 1952, 1953 and 1954 and only two of those matches, both at home to France, could be classified as narrow defeats.

Yet as Wales had signalled the start of the losing run, so did they mark the Scotland recovery. On February 5, 1955, after four years and two days without a win, Scotland beat Wales 14-8, having trailed 3-0 at half-time. This was followed by a second win, against France, but the decade continued to be grim for Scotland. They won the wooden spoon in 1956 and 1959 and it would take them until 1984 before they won the championship again.

# 10

## Scotland 10 South Africa 68. 1997

**E**ngland were not the only side to receive a walloping from southern hemisphere opposition at the back end of the 1990s (see The Worst Defeats). Eight months before Clive Woodward's team went on a tour to hell, Scotland had their own diabolical tormentors come and damn them in their own back yard. The Murrayfield massacre, like many true wallopings, came straight out of the blue. South Africa led by only 14-3 at half-time but the shackles came off after the break.

Percy Montgomery was the main destroyer. Not only did he score two of South Africa's ten tries, but he also converted eight of them. The Springboks' tries came from forwards and backs alike, everyone desperate to get their hands on the ball. James Small, the right wing, got two tries for himself and each member of the back row, Gary Teichmann, Andre Venter and Johan Erasmus, picked up one, showing the dominance they had at the breakdown.

Was this perhaps South Africa's revenge mission for losing that summer to the Lions? The Murrayfield massacre was the sixth match in what would be a 17-game winning streak, which featured some equally hefty margins of victory: 61-22 v Australia, 62-31 v Italy and 96-13 against Wales. But the win against Scotland was particulary wounding and with each try that his side ran in, was Teichmann, the captain, perhaps thinking "That's for the Lions" after the winning team had been coached by two Scots in Jim Telfer and Ian McGeechan?

This match was also notable for being the debut of Gordon Bulloch, the hooker and future Scotland captain who went on two Lions tours. "There was no celebrating afterwards," he said of his debut. Quite. No doubt everyone's bodies were aching too much.

# CHAPTER TEN

# The Worst of Wales

# 1 Llanelli's bad luck

Despite Wales's success in the Six Nations Championship over the past decade, Welsh clubs have struggled in the Heineken Cup and the only time one reached a final up to 2008 was when Cardiff were beaten in extra time by Toulouse in the very first European final, 12 years earlier. But Llanelli have come as close as any other Welsh side and could have reached the final on several occasions if it wasn't for some outlandish bad luck.

The worst of these was in the pool match against Gloucester in 2001.

Unbeaten to this point, Llanelli travelled to Kingsholm knowing that one more win would ensure them a place in the quarter-finals and despite the jeering from the home fans in "The Shed" they roared into a 13-0 lead. But Gloucester were given a penalty try when Llanelli pulled down a maul and Simon Mannix, the fly half, kept kicking penalties to keep the game in the balance.

With two minutes remaining, Llanelli led 27-25 but for the second year in a row they were denied by cruel fate. In 2000, it was Paul

Grayson's last-minute penalty in the semi-final that broke Welsh hearts. This time it was the strangest of dropped goals for Elton Moncrieff. As the clock ticked down, the Gloucester scrum half attempted a dropped goal, but it was not a good kick, on too low a trajectory, and should have missed. It would have done if it hadn't ricocheted upwards sharply off a Llanelli forward. Some said it was Dafydd Rees-Jones's back, others saw it as the shoulder of Phil Booth. Either way, the ball struck a Welshman and bounced up and over the crossbar. Gloucester won 28-27 and Llanelli were out.

Their bad luck was not quite done, either. A year later they played Leicester in the semi-finals, having beaten them in the pool stages, and were leading by two points in the last minute when Tim Stimpson attempted a desperate penalty goal from 58 metres. The ball bobbled and wobbled and never looked like making it until it suddenly hit the crossbar and flipped over. Three games, three terrible late defeats for Llanelli.

# 2 Four losses out of four

The 1990 Five Nations Championship is memorable for supporters of both Scotland and Wales. The Scots won the grand slam, triple crown and Calcutta Cup in one fell swoop at Murrayfield, while England, the vanquished in that final match, had shown the signs of brilliance that would lead them to three grand slams in the next five years and the World Cup final. For Wales, however, 1990 was a year to forget.

Never before had the men in red shirts gone through a Five Nations season without a win. Even coming last was something of a rarity. They were last in 1989 but had at least beaten England in Cardiff. The only other occasions since the war when they came at the back of the field were in 1949, 1963 and 1967. But in 1990, they hit rock bottom.

It began in Cardiff with a 29-19 defeat by France, got far worse with a 34-6 loss at Twickenham and then the wooden spoon was sewn up with two narrow defeats against Scotland and Ireland. As former Wales greats queued up to profess their despair on television, those golden days of the

1970s seemed a long way away. So, in fact, did the 1987 World Cup, when Wales had come third.

What went so wrong? Simply, the country had lost its way. The retirement of several leading players after the 1987 World Cup was compounded by the aggressive poaching of the top stars from rugby union by a resurgent rugby league. The signing of Jonathan Davies, the exciting young fly half, by Widnes particularly broke Welsh hearts but who could blame him when Widnes were offering £225,000 a year and the rugby union governing bodies were still stubbornly preventing players from earning money from their sport?

Wales almost lost all four matches again in 1991, with only a 21-21 draw with Ireland saving their blushes, but they conceded 72 more points than they scored in the three other games. They came last again in 1993, but gradually, with talented youngsters like Neil Jenkins and Scott Gibbs coming through, Wales began to reassert themselves. With grand slam titles in 2005 and 2008, few even remember that the early 1990s was so barren.

# 3  Kembery sees red

**A**ndrew Kembery, a 6ft 8in Neath lock, never played for Wales despite many advancing his claims, but he nonetheless holds two notable records. In 1990 he became the youngest player to appear in a Welsh Cup final and the first to receive a red card in one.

The incident 16 minutes into the second half at Cardiff Arms Park soured a glorious season for Neath, who had already won the unofficial Welsh Championship and the Merit Table (it was the days before wholly official leagues) and were leading 12-7 against Bridgend in the cup final when Kembery decided to dance the fandango at the base of a Neath ruck. Oddly, it was one of his own team-mates, rather than a Bridgend player, on whom Kembery's studs rained down, but it was nonetheless reported to the referee, Clive Norling, by one of the touch judges and Kembery was dismissed for stamping.

Bridgend took advantage of Neath's momentary despair to draw to within two points after a dropped goal by Aled Williams, but Kembery's team-mates regrouped and finished the match the stronger side. Chris Bridges, the scrum half, scurried over to score a try two minutes from time that ensured a 16-10 win.

The repercussions for Kembery were more serious than simply some teasing back in the dressing room after the game and rebuking headlines. It also cost him a place in the Wales side. Ron Waldron, the Neath coach who had been given the unenviable task of rebuilding the Wales team after a miserable couple of seasons, dropped Kembery from the Wales squad to tour Namibia. He made it as far as the Wales A side a couple of years later, but beset by a string of injuries he never did get to pull on the red jersey.

# 4  Gwynn takes eye off the ball

**The Gwynn brothers, William and David, were Swansea's first sporting superstars. Both** played rugby for Wales, although not at the same time, and cricket for Swansea. William would hold office as the Welsh Rugby Union's first paid secretary and he was the Welsh representative on the International Rugby Board. He was also a soccer referee.

Yet for all the good he did for sport, it is for a moment of idiotic show-boating that William Gwynn earns his place in this collection. It was 1884, the second year of the International Championship, which became the Five Nations with the later addition of France, and Wales were still trying to find their feet in a sport that England and Scotland had been playing at international level for a decade longer. Wales, having won only one of their first four internationals, played host to Scotland in Newport and Gwynn, a twinkle-toed half back, had seemingly put Wales ahead when he changed direction at speed with ball in hand and cut through the Scotland defence to cross the line.

The sensible thing to do at that point would be to put the ball down and accept the applause of the crowd, but Gwynn was so chuffed with the way in which he had left the Scotland defenders standing that he stopped and looked around for a teammate to see if anyone else wanted to touch the ball in the Scotland in-goal area. Unfortunately for him, the delay proved fatal. The chasing Scotland defenders pounced on him and the ball came loose. Wales did not score a point throughout the rest of the game and were beaten by one goal.

Incidentally, it was another moment of controversy in that year's championship that led to the creation of the International Rugby Board on which Gwynn would later sit. In the match between England and Scotland, play was held up for ten minutes while the referee debated with the players about the legality of England's try. Scotland later protested at the RFU being the sole interpreters of the laws and so the IRB was set up as an independent rules body.

# Double blow in 1980

**B**ill Beaumont's grand slam-winning England side in 1980 was based on an uncompromising set of forwards who gave as good as they got in the dark arts of rugby. Having won the first two matches of the Five Nations that year, hopes were rising that this might be the year. They had not won the grand slam since 1957 and not even the championship since 1963. But before celebrations could begin there was the small matter of a match against Wales, still in their pomp, at Twickenham.

It was a tough game that began rough and got rougher. The first lineout was a brawl rather than a contest and the game was only five minutes old when David Burnett, the referee, pulled the captains aside and warned them that the next player to offend would be off for good. Only a few minutes later, Paul Ringer, the Wales flanker, poleaxed John Horton, England's fly half, with a stiff-arm tackle across the face and was given his marching orders. Ringer, who would play only once more for Wales, was the first man to be sent off at Twickenham for 55 years.

The game degraded from there. Thirty-four penalties were awarded, two thirds of them against Wales, who many felt were the better team on the day if only they could have put as much attention into maintaining possession as they did to throwing punches. In the end, the match was decided by a moment of idiocy by Elgan Rees, the wing.

England led 6-4 with three minutes remaining when Alan Phillips, the Wales hooker, charged down an attempted clearance by Steve Smith and Rees grabbed the ball and ran towards the corner. A converted try would have put Wales more than a penalty ahead, but instead of running round and grounding the ball between the posts to make the conversion easy, Rees charged at the corner and placed the ball down there.

The conversion was missed, meaning Wales led 8-6, and in the dying seconds England were awarded a penalty goal on the touchline. Dusty Hare stroked the ball between the uprights as if it had been in front and England's grand slam dream was still on the tracks.

# 6

# The dullest game?

**F**ebruary 1963 was a terrible month for supporters of flowing rugby and not just because it was a bitter winter. In four matches in the Five Nations Championship a combined aggregate of 20 points was scored. Ireland drew 0-0 with England and lost 3-0 to Scotland, either side of a 6-5 "thriller" in which England beat France, but it was the opening match of the month that received the most criticism for being boring and eventually led to a change in the rules of the game.

Wales were playing Scotland at a wet, cold and muddy Murrayfield – not the best conditions for running rugby – and their strategy was simple: if they couldn't run with the ball, they would just kick it continuously instead. The rules in those days allowed players to kick directly into touch from anywhere on the field and retain the throw-in at the line-out, which Wales exploited to the full.

Clive Rowlands, a teacher by day and a Pontypool scrum half in his own time, was the main architect of the strategy in what was only his second international, having been made captain on his debut. Time and again, whenever Rowlands got the ball he hoofed it out of touch downfield and hoped that Wales would win it back. There were 111 lineouts in the match, one every 43 seconds, and by choking Scotland of possession Wales won 6-0, with Rowlands scoring three of the points by a dropped goal. It gave Wales a rare win in a championship in which they finished last.

The match was described as "the ultimate in non-handling rugby", but it prompted the International Rugby Board to change the laws and make it illegal to kick directly to touch except from within your own 25 (now 22). Rowlands was given the nickname "Clive the Kick" after that match and certainly the strategy ran counter to the attacking philosophy he espoused as coach of Wales a decade later.

# Miss, miss, miss...

**A**nyone can miss a kick at goal. Many very fine players have missed kick after kick. Let it not be forgotten that Jonny Wilkinson missed four dropped goals in the 2003 World Cup final before getting one over that mattered. But you have to feel sorry for a player on his debut who misses five consecutive penalty goals, especially when the match is against your team's oldest rivals and the game is scoreless.

Kel Coslett was a young full back for Aberavon, a week past his 20th birthday, when he was asked to play for Wales against England at Twickenham in 1962. It was the first match of that year's Five Nations and having come second to France the year before Wales needed a good start to begin their challenge for a first title since 1956. Coslett already had a reputation as a conscientious kicker and when he missed his first pop at goal, the ball perhaps caught by the swirling winds at Twickenham where one end was still open, he just got his head down and took more time over the next kick.

The trouble is that he kept on missing kicks and kept on taking longer over the next one. In all, he missed five penalty goals, the last of which took him 75 seconds to complete. With England showing no attacking skill of their own, the match ended 0-0 and the authorities soon ruled that attempted kicks be limited to 60 seconds, a rule that Neil Jenkins, Coslett's descendant at full back in the 1990s, always seemed to stretch.

Coslett played two more times for Wales in rugby union, and finally got some points (three of them) in his last match, but he decided afterwards that his future lay in rugby league. He signed for St Helens that season, where he stayed until 1976. Naturally, he became known as one of the finest goal-kickers the club had ever seen. In 1963, he scored points in every game but one for St Helens and topped the kicking table. What Wales would have given if just one of those had come at Twickenham the previous year.

# 8 Bassett's allsorts

**P**ast glories count for nothing when you have made a fool of yourself captaining your country. Jack Bassett was a successful full back for Penarth, who won 15 caps for Wales (nine as captain) and was selected for the 1930 Lions tour to Australia and New Zealand, on which he did so well that the *Daily Telegraph* in 2008 nominated him as a candidate for one of the best Lions full backs ever.

In 1931, Bassett captained Wales to their first Five Nations Championship since 1922, with wins over France, Scotland and Ireland and a draw at Twickenham, but the first signs of his mercurial side were seen in the Wales match against South Africa that autumn when his risky passing and poor decision-making were blamed for South Africa's 8-3 win. Nonetheless, Bassett was asked to lead Wales again in the 1932 championship and after wins against England and Scotland, Wales just needed to beat Ireland at home for the grand slam (France being absent that year).

It was not to be and the blame was pinned on Bassett. First, he dropped the ball inside his own 25, letting Edward Lightfoot, the Ireland wing, run in to score. He later failed in his job as last line of defence as Shaun Waide ran in a try from 80 yards out, rounding Bassett with ease. Few cared to remember that two years earlier Bassett's defence against Ireland, when he stopped three tries with his tackling, was impeccable.

But the game was not up: with minutes remaining, Dicky Ralph received a long pass from Wick Powell, the scrum half, and jinked through a static Ireland defence to score under the posts. That made the score 12-10 to Ireland and with an easy conversion to come Wales could secure the title even if they could not win the grand slam.

Up stepped Bassett, away went the ball... but he missed. Ireland won and the championship honours were shared. Bassett never played for Wales again.

# 9  Bush wilts under pressure

**F**ew sportsmen are given the chance to tweak the noses of the greatest of their day. If the chance comes, you had better not waste it as poor Percy Bush did in 1905. Bush was a talented fly half for Cardiff who is something of a rarity because he was selected for the 1904 Lions tour to Australia and New Zealand without having played for Wales first. He took part in four of the Tests on that tour and built a reputation for his elusive running. The Australian press called him "Will o' the Wisp".

His national debut came in December 1905, when he played in the controversial Wales win over the mighty touring All Blacks (see Worst of Referees). That was New Zealand's first defeat in 28 matches on their tour of the northern hemisphere and having beaten Glamorgan and Newport after the loss they returned to the Cardiff Arms Park on Boxing Day bent on revenge. The ground was packed, with some 50,000 spectators estimated, and Cardiff took an early 5-0 lead after a try by Gwyn Nicholls, the centre. New Zealand were then reduced to 14 men when Jim O'Sullivan broke his collarbone (in those days, there were no replacements).

The All Blacks countered hard, drawing level on the stroke of half-time through a try by Mona Thomson, and so the score stayed for the first 30 minutes of the second half before Bush's moment of calamity. Charles Seeling, the New Zealand flanker, hacked the ball downfield and it rolled across the Cardiff line, with Bush there ready to tap it down for the drop-out. Yet for some reason he delayed. Maybe he wanted to taunt the chasing New Zealanders. Maybe he just felt he had more time. But for some reason, he delayed and then decided to kick the ball clear. Alas, his boot missed the ball altogether and before he knew it George Nicholson was up on him and had grounded the ball for a try.

It was converted, giving New Zealand a 10-5 lead, and although Cardiff pulled back a try themselves they could not convert it, meaning New Zealand had won 10-8. It was Cardiff's only loss of the season. The next year they beat South Africa 17-0. Bush was at least forgiven by the Wales selectors, who picked him for seven more Tests.

# 10

## Wales beaten by Welshman

**If only Alan Rees had stayed in Llantrisant rather than emigrating to British Columbia, would Welsh** rugby in the early 1990s have been so dire? It was Rees's son Gareth, a proud Canadian, who inflicted one of their most humiliating defeats on Wales during a pretty grim period for the men in red, kicking 16 of Canada's 26 points in a 26-24 win in Cardiff in 1993.

That year was almost as depressing for Welsh rugby fans as 1990 had been (see earlier in this chapter). Despite a 10-9 win over England in the spring's

Five Nations, they lost their other three matches (the away games against France and Scotland were quite one-sided) and by the end of the tournament the Welsh rugby union was back to squabbling and infighting again. The entire general committee was sacked after a vote of no confidence by the clubs.

There was a false dawn that summer when Wales had a successful tour to southern Africa, followed by a comfortable win over Japan, but hopes of a renaissance of Welsh fortunes were swiftly shattered that November by the visit of Canada.

Canada have been playing rugby since 1932 and have qualified for every World Cup but despite a few good results in the early 1990s they were not expected to beat a strong Wales side on home soil. The oddest thing about Canada's win was that Wales, with Ieuan Evans and Scott Gibbs in the threequarters, could not cross the tryline once. If it wasn't for the metronomic kicking of Neil Jenkins, who set an international record of eight penalty goals, Wales wouldn't even have been in the game.

As well as Rees's penalties, Canada scored two tries, the first through Ian Stuart, the captain, and then with 40 seconds to go they scored a second, the ball passing from wing to wing before Al Charron, the lock, barged his way over. That made it 24-24 and Rees had the chance to secure a famous win. If there were any Reeses remaining in Llantrisant, they probably chose that moment to go away and make a cup of tea or something stronger.

# CHAPTER ELEVEN

# The Worst of France

# 1

# France v New Zealand, 2007

**J**o Maso, the long-serving France manager with the Shirley Valentine haircut, must have been wondering whose bright idea it was to arrange a summer tour to New Zealand before their home World Cup started. Sure, beating the All Blacks in their own back yard can be a tremendous boost just before a global tournament – look at England in 2003 – but France were not likely to win and the chance of a morale-sapping embarrassment was high. Furthermore, New Zealand were on a run of 21 straight home wins, one behind England's record streak at Twickenham from 1999-2003, and they were hardly in the mood to stop winning.

Just to add to the sense of foreboding about French chances, the touring side were not allowed to field their best players because the tour clashed with the final two weeks of their domestic season. As a result, Bernard Laporte, the France coach, named 14 uncapped players in his 26-man squad, 11 of whom were picked for the first match of their Test series with the All Blacks in Auckland. The words lambs and slaughter come to mind.

New Zealand, with star names

from prop to full back, were expected to win with ease but the margin of victory and the way they collapsed after the interval was concerning for France. Aaron Mauger scored first and Sitiveni Sivivatu grabbed a second try just before half-time after a chip-through, but although Jean-Francois Coux pulled one back for France there were three more tries for the All Blacks, who played 40 minutes without two of their best players, Dan Carter and Richie McCaw, who had picked up knocks. They also, as happens with winning sides, got the rub of the green a couple of times, with the referee missing a couple of New Zealand knock-ons. The margin of 42-11 was pleasing but not perfect for New Zealand.

A week later, however, France were blown off the park in Wellington. New Zealand scored nine tries and dominated in all departments to set a new world record of 23 straight home wins. The game was gone at half-time as they led 30-3 and further tries after the break sealed a record 61-10 win. Of course, what did any of this matter after France knocked New Zealand out of the World Cup six months later?

# 2  How's that for openers?

It is always crucial to get off to a strong start in the pool stages of a World Cup, especially when you are playing in front of your home crowd. England could not do it in 1991, when they lost to New Zealand at Twickenham, and while that didn't ultimately prevent them reaching the final it could have proved a fatal blow to their confidence. For France in 2007, it was even more imperative to win the tournament opener against Argentina. With Ireland, in good form, also in their group and only two teams progressing, one of the big sides would be going home prematurely.

Eighty minutes into the tournament and it looked as if that side could be the hosts. Argentina's winning margin may have been only five points in a 17-12 victory, but the manner of their win was embarrassing for France. Error followed error as France let their nerves get to them. The intensity of Argentina from the kick-off stunned France and silenced the partisan crowd. Juan Martín Hernández, the Argentina fly half, was attempting dropped goals from the start and while two attempts sailed wide Argentina were soon on the scoresheet with a penalty by Felipe Contepomi.

David Skrela got France back in the game with a penalty, but Argentina kept pushing forward, their aggressive pack forcing silly mistakes from France. Another penalty ensued and a third – as well as a third missed dropped goal – before a rare France attack ended with Rémy Martin's pass being intercepted by Contepomi, who sent Ignacio Corleto haring away to the corner for the try that gave Argentina a 14-3 lead. That became 17-9 at half-time after an exchange of penalties.

France needed to start the second half strongly and they did, but a rumbling driving maul was resisted. It took almost 20 minutes before Skrela, who missed some kicks, came good with his fourth penalty to narrow the gap to within a score. But if anyone could have stolen the game in the last quarter it was Argentina, with Contepomi spilling a try-scoring pass and missing two penalties. France looked for the crucial try, but the Pumas' defence held firm. Afterwards Bernard Laporte, the French coach, could only quote Asterix. "The sky has fallen on our head," he said.

# 3  France v England. 1992

The theory that the French dash between beautiful and suicidal, always with a finger hovering over the self-destruct button, has been around for decades but in the early 1990s, when the phrase Le Crunch was trotted out each year, it was more likely than not that part of England's training schedule would include a dossier entitled "Operation: Wind-Up".

Brian Moore, the pugnacious hooker, was the chief tormenter, a man who believed in what Steve Waugh, the former Australia cricket captain, called "mental disintegration".

Every year, Moore would be chirruping away before the big match about the failings he had spotted in the France team and then reminding them of those comments as the game progressed. More often than not, it worked.

The apotheosis of this strategy in action came in the 1992 match in Paris. The previous year, England had beaten France in a breathtaking grand-slam decider at Twickenham. Now France wanted revenge. My, how they wanted it. As their front row packed down near the end, you could see the tears streaming down their players' faces, the veins bulging on their foreheads. No doubt Moore picked that moment to have a chirrup.

So long as Philippe Sella, the France captain, was on the field there was a chance that the game would not descend into anarchy. Sella was a calm, rational man. But when he had to come off after an accidental clash of heads with Rob Andrew, hell broke loose. England led 18-7 at the time; they went on to win 31-13. This margin was helped no doubt by France having two men – Gregoire Lascube and Vincent Moscato – sent off. Some felt they were lucky only to lose two. Gouging, punching and testicle-twisting became France's attacking weapon in the scrum rather than the shove. Pity poor Stephen Hilditch, the Irish referee, for having to enforce order.

Lascube, a police inspector in his day job, was dismissed for stamping on Martin Bayfield's head; Moscato for head-butting at the scrum. Neither was quite as farcical as Jean-Luc Sadourny and Alain Penaud running into each while going for the same ball. It summed up the day of chaos.

# France v England.
## 1993

**T**he year after the battle of Paris, a more disciplined France won the Five Nations Championship with wins over Scotland, Wales and Ireland, but it could and should have been a clean sweep and the grand slam if they hadn't had the worst of luck in yet another match against England. It was England's sixth consecutive win against France, a record they would stretch to eight matches before losing at home in 1995. This time, their main weapon was not Brian Moore's mischievous tongue but the woodwork.

England did not look like they had the slightest chance of scoring a try until the France upright came to their aid. Jon Webb, the full back who had a pretty ropey game all afternoon, was given a penalty late in the first half on the left-hand side of the field and again he failed to slot the ball between the posts. Instead it ricocheted off the left post and rebounded in the direction of Ian Hunter, who had the presence of mind to follow the ball. Maybe he and Webb had been practising.

The ball fell so sweetly for Hunter that he caught it at waist height without needing to break his stride. It was the simplest of runs to the line as the French watched in amazement. They had scored two tries, both for Philippe Saint-Andre, but now they were about to go in at the break 13-12 down.

Webb added three more points in the second half, as did Didier Cambérabéro for France, but the home side clung on to their one-point margin. Again the woodwork was to benefit them. Cambérabéro and Aubin Hueber both hit the crossbar with dropped goal attempts. If either had gone over, France would have won the grand slam. It is a surprise that wood hasn't been preserved in the Twickenham museum.

# 5

# France v England.
# 1985

**Y**es, another moment of horror for Les Bleus in a game against the old enemy. This was another close game that fate cruelly took away from the French, although on this occasion they did at least escape with a draw. By failing to win, however, France were ultimately denied the championship title.

Patrick Esteve was the culprit. A speedy wing who was given the nicknames the Narbonne Express and Le TGV, Esteve won 25 caps between 1983 and 1988, scoring a try every other game. Two years earlier, he had scored in France's 19-15 win over England and a second try against the men in white was beckoning when, with England leading 3-0, the ball was quickly passed out to Esteve on the right.

That the final pass from Philippe Sella was noticeably forward is by the by. Esteve pinned his ears back, wheeled his legs and managed to escape the attentions of Rory Underwood to cross the line at pace. Knowing it would be a close game, Esteve sprinted round towards the posts to give his fly half a more easy conversion. He was in full celebration mood, barely paying attention. Certainly he did not see the figure of Richard Harding, the scrum half,

come tearing round and grasp him before he could put the ball down. Harding tucked his left arm round man and ball and, as Esteve desperately tried to touch down, the ball wriggled loose.

France did not come close to scoring another try. In fact, they felt quite hard done by in the second half as the referee, David Burnett, awarded 15 penalty kicks against them and only one in their favour. Rob Andrew took his chances where he could and England snatched a 9-9 draw.

# 6

## France v Ireland.
## 1985

**P**erhaps France's players were still fuming after the one that had got away a month earlier against England (see previous entry), but when they travelled to Lansdowne Road they still had a chance of winning the title if they could only beat Ireland. A disciplined, controlled performance was in order. Sadly it was not to be.

Observers felt that France should have won this game if only they had been more concerned with winning the ball than winning the punches; if only they did not regard penalty decisions against them as a job hazard, rather than something shameful. According to Jacques Fouroux, the France coach, it was all the fault of the referee. Kerry Fitzgerald, from Brisbane, must be biased because he spoke

English. Never mind all the illegal moves France used to win the ball, or their umpteen forms of obstruction.

Of the penalties given to Ireland, seven were kickable and Michael Kiernan succeeded with five of them to set up a 15-15 draw. It was the Cork centre's first game as Ireland's designated kicker, having taken over the duties from Ollie Campbell. He went on to score 308 points and become Ireland's record scorer.

This was the second match of Ireland's attempt to win a first grand slam since 1948. Their opening game against England was postponed by snow, but after beating Scotland, the Irish needed to beat France to maintain momentum. The draw hurt them as much as it hurt the French, therefore. Ireland went on to beat England and Wales, securing a triple crown, but they could have done with one more act of generosity from France to get the grand slam in the bag. It would be the last championship that Ireland would win until 2009. France, by contrast, soon bounced back, winning the title the next year.

# 7  Brive v Pontypridd. 1997

In many ways 1997 was a great year for Pontypridd. League champions of Wales for the first and only time, they had won the Welsh Cup the previous season and were in good form in the Heineken Cup. But their trip to Brive, the defending European champions, in the Limousin region is one that they would rather forget.

The bare facts of the match itself are that Patrick Lubungu scored a try in the dying seconds to regain the lead and ensure a Brive win. But those who came to the Stade Amédée-Domenech to see a boxing match may have been disappointed by such evidence of rugby. That surely was not the point. The game was only 27 minutes old when a mass punch-up broke out that involved 27 of the 30 players. It is surprising that only Dale McIntosh, the Ponty No 8, and Lionel Mailler, the Brive flanker, were sent off.

Since the afternoon fight had ended in a draw, it was decided to continue the brawl in a local bar, Le Touzac, that evening. Opinions differ on who started the fight. The French claimed that Ponty supporters had arrived spoiling for a fight after losing the match. The Welsh said that a Frenchman had thrown the first bottle. Either way, it was a good old-fashioned fight and one that the French came off worst in. Christophe Lamaison and Philippe Carboneau had their noses broken. Another Frenchman had both eyes blackened. Eventually the gendarmerie had to send in the riot control police with tear gas to split the sides up. "It was like being in a Western," Lamaison said. Three Ponty players were arrested, but the organisers of the match decided to fine both sides. Again, it ended in an unsatisfying draw, but Brive were the ultimate winners as having won the game they made their path to a second final in a row, losing to Bath by one point.

# 8 Toulouse blow the cup final

Those who, like the author of this book, were sat in the diagonally opposite corner of Twickenham when Rob Howley scored the try that won the Heineken Cup final for London Wasps in 2004 were scratching their heads about what had happened. Somehow, in a match that seemed to be heading for extra time, Wasps had scored a try from nowhere and were in the lead against Toulouse. What was going on?

Toulouse had taken the lead after seven minutes with a penalty. When Wasps kept pulling down the scrum, Toulouse were given another penalty, which they scored. Wasps got the first try of the game, however, with Howley bringing play back into midfield and handing Stuart Abbot a scoring pass. Wasps went ahead 13-6, but Yann Delaigue brought his side back to within two with a chip ahead and score in the right corner.

Mark Van Gisbergen scored at the start of the second half, but Toulouse dominated the territory and kept on totting up points, even if they could not score tries. The score was 20-20 with the clock ticking off its final moments and Toulouse had a 22 drop-out to restart play, but it was a loose, lazy kick and Howley, the veteran Wales scrum half, countered straight away, sending a grubber kick down the left touchline to test the French defence.

Quite what was going through the mind of Clément Poitrenaud, the full back, is not clear but he appeared to be caught in two minds about whether to take the ball into touch or the in-goal area or even whether he should pick it up and start an attack. Eventually, the ball ran dead and Poitrenaud decided to touch it down for another 22 drop-out but Howley had followed up his kick and dived at the Frenchman's feet to touch the ball down. After a long wait for the TV referee's confirmation, the try was given. Just to add to Toulouse's annoyance, Van Gisbergen's conversion crept over via the bar. It just wasn't their day.

# 9   A fallow year

**F**rance have dominated the Heineken Cup since its first season in 1995-96. French clubs have won it four times (Toulouse three and Brive one) but have had eight losing finalists, including Perpignan in the all-French final of 2003, and they have had perennial semi-finalists and quarter-finalists.

This came to an end in 2009, when only one side, Toulouse, reached the quarter-finals (at which point this book went to press) and even Toulouse's presence appeared in doubt until the final game of the pool matches. They needed to beat Bath at the Rec to be certain of qualifying as one of the best runners-up, but on a wet and muddy day the natural attacking instincts of both sides were curtailed and the game ended 3-3. Fortunately for Toulouse, the earlier result of another

French club, Castres, who beat London Wasps, gave them a second life.

It was one of only two wins for Castres in the Heineken Cup that season, so their progression was never a question. But every other French side, bar Toulouse, struggled. Clermont Auvergne, Stade Francais and Biarritz, three stalwarts of the competition, won only half their six games, while Perpignan won two out of six and Montauban just one.

It was the first time in the competition's history when only one of the last eight teams was French. Most seasons they have had three quarter-finalists – and in 1999 it was four – but it appeared that many clubs placed their priority on playing in the Top 14, the French domestic championship, rather than the European Cup. The sole progression of Toulouse followed a downward trend, with only two French sides going through in the past two years.

Philippe Saint-Andre, the former France captain and director of rugby at Sale Sharks, denied that there was a crisis, but perhaps he could say that: he had brought three of France's best players over to play for him in Stockport.

# 10 Germany? Really. Germany?

**M**ercurial France have generously given some surprising victories to teams over the years. As well as the usual suspects, France have lost to Romania eight times – and drawn twice – in their 49 encounters. Almost all of these were in Bucharest when Romania was a properly funded side playing under communism, sport being one of the few things that thrived in those days. Yet there was also an embarrassing 12-6 loss at home in Auch in 1990 when a weakened, but still not weak (it included Serge Blanco, Philippe Saint-Andre and Didier Cambérabéro),

France side was put out.

France did not have a bad side either when they lost 20-16 away to Tonga in 1999. The backs featured the likes of Jean-Luc Sadourny, Philippe Bernat-Salle, Christophe Lamaison and Fabien Galthie. The forwards were less established but there were two future France captains who came off the bench in Raphael Ibañez and Fabien Pelous. Tonga scored three tries for their only win to date against one of the original Five Nations. They have also beaten Italy once.

Those losses are just about defensible given that they are

established rugby nations who have competed in World Cups. It is also okay for France to have a loss against the United States on their record as it was during the Olympics more than 80 years ago. But Germany?? This is where I struggle.

Germany have an Olympic silver medal to their credit in 1900, although they played only one match, losing to France, and thus were given the runners-up prize, but their pedigree begins and ends there. They only started playing international rugby in 1927 and their opportunities were restricted. Great Britain refused to play them, for a start. Germany have played at Twickenham once, however, losing 26-8 there to Harlequins in 1956.

So their main competition before the war was against the other countries of continental Europe. Actually, they did not do badly, with unbeaten records against Spain, Belgium and the Netherlands. But you would still have expected France to beat them every time. In fact, they lost twice, in 1927 and 1938, both times in Frankfurt. Eighteen months after the latter game the two countries were at war. They have not played since. France probably don't want to risk it.

# CHAPTER TWELVE

# The Worst of the Southern Hemisphere

251

#  Labuschagne cracks

**A**h, remember the days when England regularly beat the giants of the southern hemisphere? Remember, in particular, that happy day at Twickenham in 2002 when Clive Woodward's team thrashed South Africa 53-3. Jonny Wilkinson probably does; he has the scars to prove it. England were leading 8-0 after 20 minutes of the match, with Ben Cohen stretching over for the first of what would be seven tries against the Springboks that day. South Africa needed every man playing to his best if they were to get back in the game. Certainly they needed every man playing full stop, but they were reduced to 14 men three minutes later when Jannes Labuschagne, a lock of very little brain from Bloemhof, took Wilkinson out with a late tackle after the fly half had cleared his lines. Labuschagne was immediately shown a red card and with a man down the men in myrtle green buckled before a formidable England pack. Will Greenwood scored the first of two tries soon after, converted by Wilkinson, who had shaken off the fuzzy feeling in his head caused by the tackle.

18-3 up at half-time, the floodgates opened for England in the second period. Greenwood got his second early in the half, but by now the kicking duties had been taken over by Matt Dawson as Wilkinson's shoulder finally began to react to Labuschagne's hit. More tries came for Neil Back, Richard Hill and Lawrence Dallaglio, each member of perhaps the best back-row unit in world rugby getting in on the act.

The Springboks claimed after the game that they were not maliciously trying to injure players, but Labuschagne was handed a 23-day ban for his assault on Wilkinson. Werner Greeff, the full back, was perhaps lucky to escape after being cited for a high tackle on Phil Christophers.

# 2  New Zealand v France. 1994

**O**utside of the World Cup, New Zealand do not do defeat against European nations. It is not their style. Certainly, if they lose one match by misfortune, they tend to make amends with the next. But in 1994, just one year before a World Cup that everyone fancied them to win (and we all know how that turned out), the Kiwis appeared fallible in their own back yard.

France, who had lost twice in that year's Five Nations, were the executioners, as they would be again in a wonderful World Cup semi-final five years later. In the first match of the series, France won 22–8, slotting over three dropped goals to make New Zealand scratch their heads. Call it an aberration. On to Auckland for the backlash.

It was a tense, tight match, fought among the

forwards as for some reason the New Zealand backs were on a walkabout day. Sean Fitzpatrick, the captain, scored a try and the All Blacks led 20–16 with two minutes to go. A close win seemed on the cards. Then they kicked possession away.

Philippe Saint-Andre, France's mercurial captain and left wing, already had one claim on the title of "scorer of the best try in rugby history" when he finished a France move that began behind their own line by Serge Blanco against England in 1991. This time, he was the creator. Picking up the ball in his own 22, Saint-Andre cut inside, running past three static New Zealand defenders before going to ground. From the ruck, the ball went through eight pairs of hands before Jean-Luc Sadourny, the full back, came flying into the line to take the scoring pass.

New Zealand pride themselves on their speed – they did, after all, have a certain Jonah Lomu in their side, who was no slouch – but France stunned them with the pace and ferocity with which they attacked. It was French flair at its most breathtaking. "It was a counter-attack from the end of the world," Saint-Andre said afterwards. It certainly felt like it for the All Blacks.

# 3  Taking defeat well

**N**ew Zealand were rated as the favourites going into the 1995 and 1999 World Cups although they had received significant defeats in the run-in to both those tournaments. In 2007, however, they really thought the trophy that they had last won 20 years earlier was already in the bag. There was justification for this confidence: New Zealand had won 25 of their previous 27 Tests going into the tournament and had a squad full of talented players all hitting their prime.

One of those was Doug Howlett, the Auckland wing who could run 100 metres in under 10.7 seconds and who was breathing down the neck of Christian Cullen to be New Zealand's leading try-scorer as the World Cup began. A hat-trick against Italy in the pool match brought him level and another try against Scotland gave him the record. He no doubt had very high hopes of lifting the Webb Ellis Cup, perhaps after getting another hat-trick of tries in the final.

What he did not foresee was the way France would play in their quarter-final match in Cardiff. New Zealand lost 20-18 with Howlett watching helplessly from the stand after being controversially omitted. No doubt he had a few harsh words for his team-mates in the dressing room afterwards.

Having seen his dreams shattered, Howlett reacted in the way any good rugby player would: he got drunk. Howlett ran up a bar tab of £11,000 and then went on the rampage in the car park of the Heathrow Hilton, jumping up and down on two cars at 3am and causing a general nuisance. Soon the police popped by and arrested him.

In the sober light of day, Howlett apologised for what he called "tomfoolery" and offered to pay for the damage. "There was drink involved, and that's not an excuse, but I do take responsibility for what I've done," he said.

# 4  Sevens heaven for England

There is leaving it late, there is snatching victory at the death and then there is really rubbing your opponents' noses in it. How's this for cheek: beating New Zealand in the final of their own tournament, in front of 40,000 baying Kiwi fans, with a try scored after the hooter has sounded. What is more, England had trailed 17-0 earlier in the game. It was the final of the Wellington Sevens in February 2009, a tournament that England had never won. In the previous year's IRB World Sevens Series, the eight-event circuit, England had finished a miserable fifth, and had been beaten in Wellington by Fiji, Wales and the lowly Cook Islands. It was not a place with happy memories for them.

But England began the 2008-09 World Series well, reaching the final of the opening event in Dubai. And in Wellington, although they had lost their final pool match to Argentina, England had demolished Fiji and Kenya in the knockout stages where they would face New Zealand, perennial champions of sevens.

The home side scored first through Paul Grant and there were further tries by Zar Lawrence and DJ Forbes to give them a 17-0 lead in the first half, but Ollie Phillips, the England captain, pulled one try back to give his team hope. Rob Vickerman added a second to leave England one score behind and when Isoa Damu, the Fijian-born flanker, broke away in the dying seconds and barged over the line after the hooter the scores were level. Ben Gollings, the leading points-scorer in sevens rugby, was never going to miss the conversion and another great Kiwi choke was put down in the book.

"The only people in the stadium who wanted us to win were our management," Phillips said of the atmosphere of playing in front of such partisan support in a stadium known as The Cake Tin. It showed remarkable character to come back from such a deficit – and perhaps a touch of traditional New Zealand cavalier behaviour.

# 5

## Australia humiliated by Lions

**R**arely has a team collapsed so badly after half-time as **Australia did at Brisbane in 1966** against a weak Lions side. "It was more than shattering," the *Daily Telegraph*'s report read, "it was humiliating." Australia trailed by 3-0 before the break but conceded 28 more points without scoring after it.

The Lions began their tour with a 60-3 win over Western Australia and followed it with a 38-11 defeat of South Australia and another straightforward win over Victoria, but their next two matches destroyed any expectations that they would have it easy in the Test series. A Combined Country XV lost 6-4, while New South Wales, who provided the bulk of the international side, held the Lions to a 6-6 draw.

No one quite knew how the Test matches would play out. Historically, the Lions did quite well against Australia but when the visiting side won the first of their two Tests by 11-8 in Sydney there were hopes that Australia could level the series in Brisbane.

Captained by Colonel Mike Campbell-Lamerton, a Scotland lock who was to drop himself in New Zealand when things went so badly, the Lions could not find a way through Australia in the first half. A penalty goal from Stewart Wilson was the only difference between the sides at the changeover. Nor did the game get better at the start of the second half. Eighteen minutes had elapsed and the score was still 3-0 before a dropped goal from David Watkins stretched the Lions' lead.

Suddenly the shackles came off. The Lions found pace and vim, running in five tries in the last 22 minutes. Long before the close the home side had stopped jeering their own team and had begun to cheer for the men in red.

The high spirits did not last long for the Lions. They moved on to New Zealand where they were trounced in all four Tests and also lost to four of the state sides. Just for good measure they were beaten by British Columbia on their way home. What does that say for the strength of Australian rugby in the mid-1960s? Yet within a year they had beaten Wales in Cardiff and become the first Wallabies side to beat the Barbarians. Funny old game.

# 6

# South Africa v USA.
# 1981

**T**his has to go down as one of the most ill-planned (planning didn't really come into it), needless, waste-of-time matches every staged. It was 1981 and the campaign by anti-apartheid protesters to get South Africa thrown out of world sport was gathering pace. Technically, contact with the republic was barred in 1977 after the Gleneagles Agreement but rugby was slow to respond to the political mood and tours continued into the 1980s.

Having lost a close-fought Test series in New Zealand that was marred (or celebrated if you will) by constant protests and barracking at the games and outside the South Africa team hotels, the Springboks were obliged by the International Rugby Board to play a three-match series in the United States on the way home, the last of which would be a full international. It was hard for South Africa to motivate themselves for this, so when it was suggested that the game be played effectively behind closed doors they readily agreed.

This match, therefore, deemed to be of importance by the IRB for the development of rugby in the USA was moved at very short notice from Bleecker Stadium in Albany, New York, to a polo ground in Glenville. So late was the decision taken that no one could find the referee in his room at the Bleecker Stadium, so the nearest official was pressganged into service. Those South Africans who weren't playing were told to hang around their hotel to draw some of the attention, while to make the game doubly secret the media and the Uniteds States RFU committee were not informed of the change.

South Africa won a one-sided match on a sloping pitch 38-7. It was estimated that the total home crowd that saw the spectacle amounted to 35 spectators, 20 policemen and one reporter who somehow got a tip-off. Or maybe he had wandered in by mistake.

# 7

# Slow to succeed

There are more appropriate names for a rugby player than Slow. Charles Slow certainly failed to live up to his name in 1931 when the pale-faced young Northampton stand off, barely out of his teens, shocked South Africa in Leicester. With a dropped goal and two tries, Slow laid the foundation for a shocking 30-21 defeat by a Leicestershire and East Midlands composite side.

It was the only match that South Africa would lose on what was a highly successful tour. They began with a 14-3 defeat of Gloucester and Somerset and ended with a 6-3 victory over Scotland at Murrayfield to seal a grand slam, having earlier beaten Wales and Ireland, both by 8-3, and England 7-0.

The Leicester game aside, there were two drawn

matches, against Devon and Cornwall and South of Scotland, but otherwise precious few near misses. They may not have put out their first-choice side against Leicester and East Midlands, but Springboks are proud men and would have hated to see their undefeated run end in the unlucky thirteenth match of the tour.

South Africa's success had been based on a style of play that involved continual kicking to touch or across field for the wings to chase. The tactic, developed by Bennie Osler, the captain, did not win them many fans but it worked. Leicester *et al* denied them this option, however, the Midland pack outplaying the Springboks in the tight and keeping possession. It sucked men in and eventually created room for Slow and the other backs to find gaps and score five tries.

Slow had to wait three years for international recognition and even then it was a brief career. He played once at fly half in 1934 against Scotland and that was that. He was killed in a car accident while serving with the RAF Volunteer Reserve in 1939.

# 8  Meads loses it

**C**olin "Pinetree" Meads is one of the legends of New Zealand rugby. The lock played 55 times for his country over 14 years from 1957-71, captaining them on occasion, and is often called the greatest All Black. He was also one of the toughest. He was reported to prepare for matches by running up and down hills in New Zealand with a sheep under each arm.

Like many locks, Meads had the reputation of being what is politely called an enforcer. In 1967, during an unspectacular 14-3 win over Scotland at Murrayfield, Meads became the second All Black to be sent off in a Test when the referee, Kevin Kelleher, objected to him aiming a kick at David Chisholm, the Scotland fly half, as he emerged from a maul. Meads actually missed the player with his attempted kick, leading to the *Daily Telegraph* reporting that "for one with Meads's world-wide reputation for robust play, this was rather like sending a burglar to prison for a parking offence". He had, however, already been warned for hot-headedness by the referee who clearly had his cards marked. It rather tarnished the final international of a successful tour for New Zealand.

Chisholm was lucky he missed. A year earlier, David Watkins, the Lions fly half, had had to be carried off after being kneed so hard by Meads, while in 1969 the lock broke the jaw of Jeff Young, the Wales hooker, with a punch.

Perhaps Meads's most notorious assault came in 1968, however, when he ended the career of Ken Catchpole, the Australia scrum half. Catchpole had made the mistake of leaving a leg waggling free outside a ruck and Meads seized upon it, ripping the player's groin muscles with the intensity of the pull. As always, the New Zealand management just smiled and said "that's our Colin".

# South Africa blanked

**D**avid Chisholm, the target of Colin Meads's swinging foot in the previous entry, was the star man for Scotland when they beat the mighty South Africa at Murrayfield in 1965. Actually, the Springboks were not all that mighty on a miserable tour that resulted in the startling analysis of played five, lost four, drew one.

There is no such thing as a bad South Africa, but this team came pretty close to earning the label with a series of surprising results in the mid-1960s. Between August 1963 and September 1965, South Africa won only three of their 13 Tests.

The brief tour of the northern hemisphere was supposed to raise morale, but instead the team just kept getting worse and worse results. It started with a famous 12-10 defeat at Thomond Park in Limerick to the Combined Irish Universities, the first time South Africa had lost to any team on Irish soil. A few days later, they had their second defeat in Ireland, losing 9-6 to the national side at Lansdowne Road, with Tom Kiernan kicking the winning penalty five minutes from time. It was South Africa's first Test defeat in the British Isles for 59 years.

On then to Scotland in a filthy mood that did not lighten when once more they lost a close match. Chisholm put over a dropped goal in the last minute to give Scotland an 8-5 victory. It was a small consolation for the 44-0 hammering the Springboks had given Scotland 14 years earlier.

The year did not get much better for them. Back in the southern hemisphere, South Africa suffered their first ever defeat in Australia, going down 18-11 in Sydney. A week later they would lose the series with a 12-8 reverse in Brisbane. On the same day as the Sydney defeat, the Junior Springboks, their development side, lost in Johannesburg to Argentina.

A black spell concluded in September in Auckland when South Africa suffered a record 20-3 defeat to New Zealand, which gave the home team a 3-1 series win. It was a bad time to be a Bok, but better years were ahead with victory in 1968 against the Lions.

# 10  The worst diplomat

John O'Neill is the chairman of Brand Sydney, a government project to promote tourism to New South Wales, but there was a spell in his previous job as chief executive of the Australian Rugby Union when he did his best to put off any Englishmen from visiting his country.

Pom-baiting is a national sport in Australia. We can take a certain level of abuse. But to get told by an official in the middle of a World Cup that "everyone hates England" and that the tournament had only been given to France to stop England having it was beyond the pale. His comments offended France as well.

"Whether it's cricket, rugby league or rugby union, we do all hate England," O'Neill said. "All I'm doing is stating the bleeding obvious." On one level, it was a funny comment that should not be taken too seriously. On another, it was a display of pettiness by a public figure who should have been more dignified. He went on: "Sadly, this is all a by-product of their born-to-rule mentality. It's been there a long time and nothing has changed." Maybe he still had a chip on his shoulder about losing the Ashes in 2005, even if they had since been regained by Australia.

His little speech was given before England played his countrymen in the quarter-final of the World Cup. A hitherto lacklustre England played above themselves to win 12-10 and knock Australia out. It was reported that the Australia coaching staff had not found O'Neill's bit of winding up the Poms helpful.

O'Neill endeared himself to another country five years earlier when he proposed to the International Rugby Board that Australia, which had originally been given joint hosting rights for the 2003 World Cup with New Zealand, should stage the tournament on their own. The IRB supported him, which made O'Neill's next trip to Auckland interesting. "I walked through the crowd at Eden Park at one point and that was an adventure," he said, adding that he was "surprisingly well recognised". Australia made a profit of $30 million from the World Cup. New Zealand have still not forgiven O'Neill for his duplicity.

# CHAPTER THIRTEEN

# The Worst of the World Cup

# 1 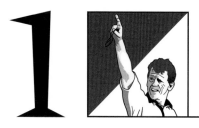 Opening anticlimax

**R**ugby union came late to the idea of World Cups. Football had been holding one since 1930, rugby league since 1954 and cricket since 1975. Rugby union contented itself, apart from four appearances in the Olympics, with the Five Nations Championship as the only multi-national tournament. An early proposal in the late 1960s to stage a union World Cup was quickly slapped down by the International Rugby Board.

As the 1980s began, the idea resurfaced and, despite initial opposition from the home nations, was accepted in 1985. South Africa's vote in favour proved critical, even though they would be banned from competing because of the apartheid boycott. So the first tournament began on May 22, 1987, at Eden

Park, Auckland, with New Zealand playing Italy.

It was not the most enticing fixture with which to start this new competition. The other pools offered matches that would have been more even (England v Australia; France v Scotland; Wales v Ireland), but New Zealand as host nation had the right to go first and it was just a shame that they had been drawn in the easiest pool. Italy had been playing international rugby since 1929 but had been given few games by the leading powers. In 1979 they had lost 18-12 to a New Zealand XV, but it was hardly the proper All Blacks. This was their first true test.

It was a gruelling initiation to grown-up rugby and a horrid anticlimax for all but the ardent home fans. New Zealand scored 12 tries and won 70-6. For their next trick, they beat Fiji 74-13. Argentina, no bad side even then, lost 46-15. It was all too easy. And it was not just New Zealand who rolled teams over. In half of the 24 pool matches in the competition, the winning side scored at least 40. World Cup rugby was on its way, but most of the world was still in the nursery.

# 2 A fight and a choke

**A**t least by the knockout stages of the first World Cup there were hopes of some close matches, although New Zealand continued their dominance into the second semi-final, where Wales were beaten 49-6. The Welsh could feel a bit unlucky as they were missing five first-choice forwards, but the match is remembered most for the unseemly fight that marked the closing stages.

With only three minutes left and the game long gone, Huw Richards, of Neath, threw a punch at Gary Whetton, the Kiwi lock. Richards was knocked semi-conscious for his efforts by Wayne Shelford and when he groggily got to his feet was told by the referee, Kerry Fitzgerald, that he could go and start running the bath. Unsurprisingly, Shelford was not sent with him – it would have taken a brave referee to tell Shelford that because of the statutory one-week ban for a red card he couldn't play in the final.

The first semi-final was a closer match that Australia rather threw away, with France the beneficiaries. The Wallabies went 9-0 up through three Michael Lynagh penalty goals, the last from 57 yards, but Lynagh missed an easy dropped goal in front of the posts to stretch the lead and Alain Lorieux scored a try against the run of play before half-time to cut the lead to 9-6.

France went ahead twice in the second half, each time being pegged back by Australian tries, but then the great Serge Blanco made a mess of a clearance on his own line to allow Australia a penalty to go 24-21 up. Back came the French again, equalising with seconds left, but fate offered the match to Australia first only for them to blink.

The ball was kicked across field by France where David Campese, the mercurial Australia wing, was lurking. It was ideal Campese territory: a burst of speed, change of pace, jink or two and he would be in. But perhaps he wasn't expecting the ball to come to him, or maybe he feared knocking it on. Either way, he hesitated and before he knew it France were on him and had turned the ball over. It went through nine pairs of hands in a flash, Blanco scored in the corner and Australia were suddenly out.

# 3 Wales lose to half an island

**N**o one knew whether it was a patronising joke or a disarmingly truthful assessment of how low they had sunk when Wales declared before their opening pool match of the 1991 World Cup against Western Samoa that it was the most important game in the 110-year history of Welsh rugby.

Western Samoa had a population of 160,000, of whom only about 2,000 played rugby. They were a developing side but had not been invited to the inaugural World Cup four years earlier.

Wales, by contrast, saw rugby more as a national religion than a national sport. They may have been on a downward slope, but they had come third at the 1987 World Cup and should have been pleased with the opposition they had been given at Cardiff Arms Park.

Western Samoa took the lead, through a penalty by Mathew Vaea, and it was 3-3 at half-time. Wales were shocked by how ferocious the Samoan tackling was – and, at times, how high and unpunished. Just as contentious was Samoa's try at the beginning of the second half. To'o Vaega kicked the ball ahead and dived to touch it down. TV replays showed that Robert Jones had clearly got there first, but the unsighted referee gave the score to Samoa. Soon after Sila Vaifale scored a less debatable try and suddenly Wales were trailing 13-3.

The men in red fought back and scored two tries of their own, through Emyr Jones and Ieuan Evans, but Vaea struck another penalty to give the visiting side a 16-13 win. The minnows had triumphed. One Welsh coach flippantly remarked that it was a good job Wales hadn't played all of Samoa.

It was no fluke. Western Samoa went on to run Australia close before losing 9-3 and then beat Argentina 35-12 before going out in the quarter-finals to Scotland. Wales, who conceded six tries to Australia, were broken. Eight years later they again played Samoa (now without the Western bit of the title) in a World Cup pool match in Cardiff. Again they lost, 38-31, but this time no one was surprised.

# 4  France take out frustration on referee

**N**o one likes losing, but France's reaction to their 19-10 defeat by England in the quarter-final of the 1991 World Cup was particularly graceless. Maybe they were just fed up with losing to England that year. In the grand-slam decider at Twickenham that spring, Philippe Saint-Andre had completed one of the finest ensemble tries, begun behind France's own goal line, but England would still win 21-19. Now, on their own turf at the Parc des Princes in Paris, France wanted revenge.

Instead they allowed themselves to get wound up by the England hooker Brian Moore, as usual in those days, and by making a string of errors they gave England chance after chance. Jonathan Webb kicked three penalty goals to go with tries by Rory Underwood and Will Carling and England won 19-10. Mickey Skinner's massive hit on Marc Cecillon, which could be felt up in the stands, shook France and they felt that the only way of getting back into the game was to turn physical. "It makes me wince when I watch it," Moore said 16 years later.

Scrappy brawls broke out and England, whose forwards played on the limit of the laws, were quite happy to incite the French. When Serge Blanco was taken out after calling a mark, the great full back felt that enough was enough and threw a rabbit punch at Nigel Heslop, the England back, who had already been thumped by Eric Champ. Meanwhile, Webb kept on kicking England towards the semi-final.

The most inexcusable act came after the final whistle. Daniel Dubroca, the France coach, walked after David Bishop, the referee, telling him what he felt of his decision and then put his hand on Bishop's chest to stop him walking away as the rant continued. "He was laughing as he walked towards the tunnel," Dubroca said. "That made me mad." Dubroca's punishment was to be asked to resign.

# 5

## Hastings misses the final

**T**wo kicks defined the first semi-final of the **1991 World Cup. One, a dropped goal by Rob Andrew at the death, gave England the lead** for the first time in the match; another, a penalty goal from in front of the posts that Gavin Hastings would have got nine times out of ten, was sliced and proved critical.

There were 20 minutes remaining when Hastings stepped up for that kick and the scores were level 6-6. He had enjoyed a good World Cup, with 56 points up to then, the last six of which had taken Scotland into an early lead at Murrayfield. They had good memories of playing England there: the previous year they had surprised many by beating the men in white in the final game of the Five Nations Championship to win a grand slam. Few would have staked money on them reaching the World Cup final, yet here they were in the first half of the semi and leading 6-0.

Jonathan Webb, the surgeon who played at full back for England, hit two clinical penalties to draw the away side level. Then came Hastings's moment of destiny. Hastings was arguably the greatest Scotland player of all time. He won 61 caps, 20 of them as captain, and scored 667 points, a national record until it was passed by Chris Paterson in 2008. He remains the all-time record points-scorer for the Lions, whom he captained in Australia in 1993, and he played a pivotal role in Scotland's 1990 grand-slam win over England. He should be remembered as a hero: instead all they talk about is one missed kick.

It was the turning point. England suddenly sprang to life, with their forwards starting to dominate the Scots. Only some brilliant, frantic defending kept England from scoring a try and on at least half a dozen occasions the England scrum appeared to be within inches of a pushover try. Scotland kept them out for as long as they could, but fate decreed that the game would go to England. Andrew's dropped goal broke a lot of hearts that afternoon.

# A dark day for the Rainbow Nation

**S**outh Africa felt it was their destiny to win their home World Cup in 1995. That was certainly the view of Louis Luyt, the head of the South Africa rugby union, who wound a few people up by saying that South Africa would have won the first two World Cups as well if they had been allowed to enter. But the path to the final was occasionally rocky and after a close but reassuring opening win against Australia, the Springboks had not looked too impressive in beating Romania 21-8.

On to Port Elizabeth for their final pool match against Canada, a modest side but capable of producing shock victories. They had, after all, been in the quarter-finals of the previous World Cup. It was the first international meeting between the teams and the atmosphere was understandably tense. If Canada won, they could knock the hosts out.

At half-time there was little chance of that, however, as South Africa showed great discipline to deny their opponents much ball while opening a 17-0 lead. That became 20-0 soon after the restart and it should have been a question of relaxing and controlling the game. Instead, the Springboks decided to have a few fights. Canada were more than up for it.

With six minutes to go the tension exploded. Winston Stanley, the Canada right wing, and Pieter Hendriks, his opposite number, decided to grapple with each other rather than contend for the ball. Scott Stewart, the Canada full back, decided to get involved and suddenly the pitch was awash with red men and green men throwing punches at each other.

It was hard for David McHugh, the referee, to work out who was most to blame. In the end none of the original three were punished there and then (although Stewart and Hendriks were later given suspensions), but McHugh did issue three red cards to Gareth Rees and Rod Snow, of Canada, and James Dalton, the Springboks hooker. It meant that Dalton missed the rest of the tournament, including South Africa's finest hour. And all for a match that his side were winning with ease.

# 7  England freak out

**W**ill Carling's assessment of the star of the 1995 World Cup was as blunt as that he had earlier given about the men running English rugby. "He [Jonah Lomu] is a freak and the sooner he goes away the better," Carling said. It was a compliment. Lomu, 6ft 5in and 19 stones, had already made his mark on the tournament with three tries as New Zealand reached the semi-final, but he had a few more up his sleeve for England.

The first of his four tries came after just 70 seconds and not from a particularly good pass. Lomu gathered the ball in the end, accelerated past Tony Underwood, fended off Will Carling and then, stumbling somewhat, ran straight over the top of Mike Catt for the line.

Not a great start by England, with Catt's effort in particular proving the lesson that optimism rarely triumphs in the face of a stampeding rhino. Worse was to come as Josh Kronfeld scored a try two minutes later and then after a series of kicks, including Zinzan Brooke, the No 8, dropping a goal, England were 18-0 down with an hour still to be played.

Lomu scored his second try before half-time – this time Rob Andrew was the soft toy he bounced off on his way to the line – and then within a minute of the restart he had his third try after Andrew Mehrtens had kicked into space and invited Lomu to chase.

England had no answer but they tried their hardest, avoiding humiliation by scoring four tries in 22 minutes, but New Zealand had already worked up a 35-point lead by the time the England fightback began and the requirement was too steep. Lomu scored his fourth try before the close, anyway, to make all England hopes about a surprising win academic.

# 8 New Zealand choke in the World Cup (again)

In 1999, the All Blacks were most people's favourites – aren't they every year? – to add a second world title to the inaugural one they won in 1987. They entered the tournament on the back of their third Tri-Nations title and waltzed through the pool stages, with Jonah Lomu, the hero of the 1995 tournament, showing that his powers had not waned by scoring five tries in three games.

Lomu scored a sixth try in the straightforward quarter-final victory over Scotland, leaving only France at Twickenham standing between New Zealand and a place in the final. It was hardly a daunting match; to that point 1999 had been a grim year for the French with only a 10-9 win over Ireland in Dublin preventing them from being whitewashed in the final Five Nations Championship.

Earlier in the year, France had lost 54-7 to New Zealand in Wellington and when Lomu scored his seventh try of the tournament in the first half of the semi-final and his eighth at the start of the second it appeared that another walloping could be on the cards for the French. But then things changed: the French scored 33 points in under half an hour to stun the would-be world champions. First it was Christophe Lamaison, who dropped two goals and kicked two penalties to cut the deficit to two. Then the famous Gallic flair kicked in.

Were New Zealand guilty of cockiness or stage fright? It looked like the latter when Jeff Wilson cut inside instead of feeding Lomu, only to lose the ball in collision with the France forwards. Fabien Galthie hacked the ball downfield, for Christophe Dominici to chase and score the try that put France in front. Four minutes later, Richard Dourthe scored and then he was followed by the silver fox, Philippe Bernat-Salles, all three tries converted by Lamaison who scored 28 of France's 43 points. New Zealand were stunned; France were in the final. They never put up a fight against Australia.

# De Beer's diamonds

**M**any of the incidents in this Worst Of... collection could easily be classified in a selection of the Best Of Rugby. One man's brilliance makes another man look foolish. New Zealand's capitulation in the 1999 semi-final to France could be presented as France's success story if it wasn't for the fact that it so comprehensively upset the form book.

Likewise, the way in which England were dumped out in the same tournament at the quarter-final stage could be put down to the sublime technical skill of Jannie De Beer or the tactical nous of his coaches. But De Beer should never have been allowed to drop an unprecedented five goals against England. His success was a result of England's failings.

Some blame Phil Larder, the new England defence coach who had arrived from rugby league with some new ideas for how to tackle. The drift defence meant that while it was harder for attacks to pierce the line, the fly half was left with a little bit more time. And De Beer decided to use that time to attempt dropped goals. Others blame England for some pretty woeful errors that kept giving South Africa the ball. In all, England committed 18 turnovers and gave away five kickable penalty goals.

What makes the heist by De Beer so frustrating is that England, who trailed 16-12 at half-time, could have won that match. Instead, with five successful dropped goals in little more than half an hour, De Beer turned the match. "I don't want to take too much credit," he said. "We had a game plan and we stuck to it. For me it was easy." Two of the kicks were made from 45 yards out.

In the semi-final, De Beer also attempted five dropped goals. But Australia's defence were wiser to it and put him under more pressure. Only one went over and Australia won 27-21.

# 10

# Barnes blights the All Blacks

**T**he Australians say that it is the Poms who whinge, but the bleating and whining that comes from New Zealand whenever one of their teams fails — again — to win the rugby World Cup can be just as loud. Wayne Barnes's mistakes in the quarter-final of the 2007 World Cup between the All Blacks and France in Cardiff may not have been particularly sinful, but the outcry that followed ensures that the referee gets his place in rogues' corner – at least as far as the Kiwis are concerned.

Barnes's elevation was swift. The youngest member of the English national panel of referees at 21, he gave up a career in the law at the age of 26 to become a professional referee and within a year was officiating in internationals. His eleventh match was that crucial quarter-final.

All was going to plan for New Zealand at half-time when they led 13-3, but France had had their chances and if three missed kicks at goal had gone over then they would have trailed by only one point. Early in the second half, Barnes sin-binned Luke McAlister, the New Zealand centre who had scored a try before the break, for illegally blocking a France player. While he was off, France drew level.

Although Rodney So'oialo's try put New Zealand back in front, Dan Carter missed the conversion and when Frédéric Michalak sent Yannick Jauzion over with 15 minutes remaining, Jean-Baptiste Elissalde added the two points to give France what would be a winning lead.

New Zealand fans later claimed that the yellow card on McAlister was harsh and that Barnes had missed a forward pass by Michalak to Jauzion. Neutrals pointed to earlier errors that had favoured New Zealand and Paddy O'Brien, the IRB's head referee and a New Zealander himself, defended Barnes, saying that he "had a decent game" and that "people have to grow up". It didn't stop death threats being made, nor the waves of abuse ahead of Barnes's next match in charge of the All Blacks.

# CHAPTER FOURTEEN

# The Worst
# of the Lions

# 1  O'Driscoll dumped out early, 2005

I n 2005, Brian O'Driscoll was at the peak of his powers. An Ireland player for six years and captain since 2003, the centre had scored 28 international tries and was an obvious choice to captain the Lions on their tour to New Zealand. He was one of 11 Irishmen in a bloated tour party of 44, coached by Sir Clive Woodward.

The tour did not begin particularly well. Having scraped a 25-25 draw with Argentina before departing – thanks to a penalty goal from Jonny Wilkinson in the eighth minute of injury time – the Lions lost their third match of the tour to the New Zealand Maori and were unconvincing in beating Wellington and Southland. They were therefore already wobbling when they lined up for the anthems, including the specially commissioned and rather ghastly *Power of Four* theme, before the first international.

Things got worse in the first minute of the game. O'Driscoll was defending at a ruck and was grabbed without the ball by Tana Umaga, his opposite number, and Keven Mealamu, the All Blacks hooker, who flipped him and drove the Irishman headfirst into the ground. As he went down, O'Driscoll stuck out an arm to protect himself and his shoulder was dislocated. O'Driscoll's tour was over before it had really begun.

Opinion was divided on the incident. The touch judge was shouting at the players to let O'Driscoll go and Woodward claimed that it was an illegal "spear tackle". An independent citing commissioner, however, ruled that there was nothing wrong with what the New Zealand pair did and that they were only clearing out the ruck. Umaga has protested his innocence and said that O'Driscoll and the Lions were milking the incident.

Certainly it took some of the attention away from the fact that the Lions were comprehensively outplayed by the All Blacks, losing 21-3. It also made it easier for them to overlook Danny Grewcock, the England lock, being suspended for two months after biting Mealamu.

# 2  Plank bites Lip. 2001

Some players should be banned from ever opening their mouth, it only ever causes trouble. In 2001, Austin Healey, the shy and retiring scrum half known as "the Leicester lip", was careless and discourteous in the way he described an opponent on the Lions tour to Australia and his words came back to haunt the side as they lost to the Wallabies for the first time.

The tour had begun so well for the Lions, too. Within three minutes of the first international, Jason Robinson had jinked his way over for the first of four tries for the Lions at the Gabba in Brisbane and a comfortable win. The series was levelled in Melbourne, however, when Jonny Wilkinson's floated pass was intercepted by Joe Roff to set up a 35-14 win. On to Sydney, where Australia called up a lock by the name of Justin Harrison.

Healey thought it would be helpful to his team-mates to write a newspaper column in which he laid into Harrison, using words such as "plod", "plank", "ape" and a few unflattering comments about Australian virility.

He later said his tactic had been to enrage Harrison into coming after him. Just one flaw: Healey got injured before the match and his team-mates bore the brunt of Harrison's wrath.

With the crucial final match entering its last 20 minutes, the game was locked at 23-23 and it was anyone's game. The Wallabies scored two penalties to move into a six-point lead, but the Lions had one more sniff of victory when Wilkinson kicked a penalty into the corner. A catch and drive over the line – followed by a conversion for dead-eye Wilkinson – would be enough to win match and series. Instead, as you could have scripted, up soared "the plank" and stole the ball to give Australia victory.

# 3 Campese's calamity. 1989

**A**sk most Englishmen to name one Australian rugby player – even one Australian sportsman – who they really can't stand, and the answer will almost inevitably be David Campese. There was something insufferably cocky about the mercurial and supremely talented wing. Was it his arrogant boasting, his disrespect even as a fresh youngster for those who had enjoyed successful careers, or simply the fact that he never missed an opportunity to call the English boring? Or was it just that he was too good?

Anyway, allow us to continue a 20-year gloat about the time when Campese was laid low by his cockiness. It was 1989 and the Lions were touring Australia for the first time in 18 years. They had never lost to Australia, but the Wallabies had a strong team and home hopes were raised after a 30-12 victory in the first international. They lost the second, meaning that everything came down to Sydney.

It was the second half and Australia were leading 12-9 when Rob Andrew, the England fly half, missed with an attempted dropped goal. Campese caught the ball behind his line and instead of touching the ball down for a drop-out decided, as was his wont, to launch a counter-attack and test the Lions stretched defence. Unfortunately, no one else was aware of this. Campese threw the ball laterally to Greg Martin, who wasn't looking, and as the ball ricocheted off Martin's shoulder, Ieuan Evans swooped in to score a try. The Lions went on to win match and series 19-18.

Campese later said, and some would agree with him, that "the idea was perfectly sound, it was just that the execution was wrong". Mark Ella, his former Australia team-mate, said that the mistake came because Campese was frustrated at not getting more of the ball. Bob Dwyer, the Australian coach, told him to forget it, that it was just one of those things, but some of his team-mates snubbed him in the dressing room and Campese's brother was thumped in a bar simply for being related to the day's hapless victim. It was psychologically wounding to Campese, but he turned that embarrassment into anger and two years later got revenge by being on the winning Australia side against England in the World Cup final.

# Toothless Lions.
## 1983

**T**he eighth Lions tour to New Zealand was one of the least successful – although the 1966 series was just a little worse. In 1983, the Lions lost all four international matches and also lost close matches to Auckland and Canterbury. They suffered from poor selection, with Paul Dodge, one of the England stars, controversially left out and a terrible list of injuries. Worst of these was poor Terry Holmes, the Wales scrum half, who was sent to hospital during the first Test in Christchurch with a torn anterior cruciate ligament, a ruptured posterior capsule of the knee and a torn medial ligament.

The most frustrating thing was that New Zealand did not have that great a side at that point in history. Later that year, they would lose to England and let slip a lead to draw with Scotland. The Lions really could have won that opening match of their series. Allan Hewson, the All Blacks full back, had a shocking match, fluffing almost every catch that came his way and appearing generally headless until, in the closing minutes, he dropped a goal from 45 yards out that secured a 16-12 win.

It would be the closest the Lions would get to winning a match. Their injury run continued, too. Nigel Melville, who replaced Holmes, lasted one game before being knocked out by a punch from an opponent in North Auckland. In the second international, New Zealand failed to add to their half-time 9-0 lead but the Lions lacked any attacking spark at all and the match finished with the same score, "a euphemism for disaster", wrote Hugh McIlvanney of *The Observer*.

After two close defeats, the Lions lost the series in the third international at Dunedin by another small margin, 15-8, at which point the All Blacks loosened their shackles and played with all the flair and creativity for which they are famous, winning the final Test 38-6.

# Lions roasting lambs. 1974

**I**f the 1983 Lions tour was one-sided against the northern hemisphere, the tour to South Africa nine years earlier was just as comprehensively won by the men in red. It was a wonderful squad who assembled under the captaincy of Willie John McBride, with no weakness in any position. Twenty-one of their 22 matches were won, with the final Test against South Africa being drawn.

The series is remembered for the physicality of the play, with McBride deciding that the best way to counter the South African dirty play and perceived bias from the home referees was to "take no prisoners". At the shout of "99", the whole team were ordered to charge into the fray, on the theory that a referee would never send off all 15 of them.

But as well as their aggression, the 1974 Lions should be remembered for the way they destroyed the South Africa forwards technically, at the scrum and in the loose. After ten minutes of the first international, Syd Millar, the Lions coach, realised that his side would win the series. They won that match 12-3, sparking panic among the South Africa selectors.

Rarely can the Springbok jersey have been so devalued. In all, 33 different players were used in the four Tests of that series by South Africa, 21 of them making their debut. The oddest selection was to respond to the injuries to Roy McCallum and Paul Bayvel, their scrum halves, with a call-up for Gerrie Sonnekus, a provincial standard No 8. Their thinking was not clear, but Sonnekus and his new team-mates had little answer to the Lions, who won the second and third Tests by 28-9 and 26-9 respectively.

The latter match was agreed to be the most violent of the tour, with the 99 call being used repeatedly. Danie Craven, the South African board president, said afterwards that he was ashamed of his players for running away so often from the Lions, yet who could blame them? The decisions taken by the selectors was proof in itself that everyone feared that Lions side.

# Swart plays without a full pack. 1974

The 13-13 draw in the final Test aside, few teams got even close to beating Willie John McBride's Lions in their rampage across South Africa in 1974. South Western Districts succumbed 97-0 in Mossel Bay, with JJ Williams scoring six tries for the Lions, Griqualand West were pushed aside 69-16 and the Leopards, a Bantu side, were beaten 56-10.

Yet one provincial side did come close to upsetting the bandwagon and if their captain had had a little more sense they may have done. It was the third minute of injury time at the end of the game and Orange Free State, captained by Jake Swart, were leading the Lions 9-7. Naturally, you didn't get into a winning position against that side without picking up a few casualties and Stoffel Botha, their lock, was barely able to walk near the end of the game, he had been so battered and bandaged up. Many felt he was even concussed.

As the referee looked at his watch again, the Lions knocked on at a lineout and Orange Free State were given one last scrum, yet instead of signalling for the doctor to have a look at Botha and possibly replace him (the decision in those days was taken by the captain, not the coach), Swart decided to let Botha sit out the crucial lineout on the sideline. Furthermore, he didn't even call up a back into the scrum, which the Lions would have seen as extreme arrogance.

You can see where this is going. The eight Lions in the scrum pushed the seven Free Staters off the ball, it was fed wide at speed to JJ Williams and the Wales wing scored in the corner. The whistle was then promptly blown, the Lions won 11-9 and their winning streak continued. And all because Swart didn't think it worth the trouble to play with a full pack.

# 7 The Battle of Canterbury, 1971

If the 1974 Lions were the toughest and most aggressive group to represent these islands, their predecessors who toured New Zealand three years earlier were arguably more exciting with a back division of JPR Williams, Gerald Davies, John Dawes, Mike Gibson, David Duckham, Barry John and Gareth Edwards.

Yet the tour got off to a disastrous start when they were beaten 15-11 in their first match in Brisbane, a stop-off in Australia on the way to New Zealand. Jetlag was blamed, but the Lions only scraped through their next match, against New South Wales, 14-12 and the All Blacks must hardly have been sleeping uneasily.

How dangerous underestimation can be. By the time the Lions had reached New Zealand they were starting to shake off their cobwebs and they embarked on a 14-match winning streak with a 25-3 win over Thames Valley. It was the ninth match of the sequence, however, that has lived on in infamy. Canterbury decided that the best way to halt the Lions was to play dirty. Fists were thrown more often than passes and the only kicking that the New Zealanders seemed interested in was at the shins of the Lions.

Among the notable injuries, Fergus Slattery lost two teeth and suffered concussion, John Pullin was knocked to the ground by a punch from behind, as was Gareth Edwards, while Ray McLoughlin, the Lions prop, deserves a little less sympathy for breaking a thumb in hitting back. Worst of all, though, was Sandy Carmichael, the Scotland prop, who suffered multiple fractures of the cheekbone. Like McLoughlin, Carmichael was sent home, leaving the Lions to begin their first Test without either first-choice prop.

The referee was unable to control the violence and eventually told the captains to get on with it and that he was only going to follow the ball. Despite that, the superior Lions backs ensured that there was no upset and they won 14-3. It only made them more determined to put one over on the All Blacks in the first Test.

# 8

# Revenge for Canterbury. 1971

**O**nly a week after being battered by Canterbury (see previous entry), the Lions had their chance for revenge in the first Test in Dunedin. They selected a glittering back division of six Welshmen and one Irishman (Mike Gibson) but it was a third-choice prop, Ian MacLauchlan, who had been called out as a replacement for Sandy Carmichael, the punchbag in Canterbury, who scored the match-winning try.

New Zealand started the match better, and must have been buoyed when Gareth Edwards, the Lions scrum half, went limping off early on with an injured hamstring, but they could not find any way through the Lions defence. However, with Barry John missing two penalty goals the match was still scoreless after 20 minutes when MacLauchlan, known as Mighty Mouse, played a crucial role. Fergie McCormick, the

New Zealand full back, was one of the chief tormentors in Canterbury and he was about to find out the meaning of the word revenge.

MacLauchlan put in a tackle on McCormick, who frantically threw the ball away in the direction of Alan Sutherland, the No 8, who was not only unprepared for the ball to come his way but was not the ideal man you wanted to kick a quick clearance. As Sutherland tried to work out which way to hold the ball, MacLauchlan came into view and, as the kick belatedly was made, the prop got his body in the way and charged it down over the line, before falling on it to score the Lions' first points. MacLauchlan grinned all the way back to the halfway line.

Yet McCormick's punishment by the fates was not over. He missed two straightforward penalties in front of the posts and was generally a gibbering wreck whenever the ball came near him. John struck two penalties to give the Lions a 9-3 win and although they would lose the second Test, they won in Wellington and drew in Auckland to seal the series win. McCormick never played for the All Blacks again.

# 9  Party like it's 1968

The 1960s were not a golden period for the Lions. Against South Africa in 1962 and 1968 and New Zealand in 1966 they lost ten matches and drew two. They did have two wins against Australia before the New Zealand leg in 1966 but it was not a good Wallabies side. Little wonder that by the end of the decade there was a fair bit of festering anger among the Lions. The innocent victims were the furniture in a series of South African hotel rooms as their post-match parties tended to get riotous. In particular, a chain of beds were broken across South Africa as those players who were awake determined not to let any team-mate sleep.

Unfortunately the 1968 tour was the first one properly covered by the media, who were keener than before to report their off-field activities. The players became known as "the wreckers" for the carnage they left behind them. At one party after they had lost the first Test 25-20, Willie John McBride, the Ireland lock and future Lions captain, managed to sustain an injury that required eight stitches in his leg and two in a finger. No one was clear quite what had happened, but he may have been practising rucking.

After they lost the third Test in Cape Town 11-6 (the second had been drawn) a really big party was needed to get rid of the disappointment. The venue was the Cape Town Hotel, run by Jeff Reynolds, a former Lion in 1938. As dawn broke, and the cleaners emerged cowering from their closets, Reynolds surveyed the carnage and totted up the cost of the damage. Being a decent sort, he halved it, then halved it again before presenting a bill for £900 to David Brooks, the Lions manager.

Brooks looked at it and then uttered the priceless comment "Huh, couldn't have been much of a party" before opening his chequebook.

# 10 Van der Schyff's shocker. 1955

**T**he tour to South Africa in 1955 was the first by a Lions party for 17 years and the home side fully expected to continue their dominant streak that went back to 1896. The Lions had lost 1-0 in 1903, 2-1 in 1910 and 1938 and 3-0 in 1924. But on this tour they did at least secure a share of the spoils, winning two of the four Tests by narrow margins, to go with two rather heavier defeats.

South Africa could and should have won the series and certainly the 90,000 fans at the first Test at Ellis Park, Johannesburg, felt that they should have gone home with a win to cheer. That they didn't was in no small part due to a terrible return to the side for Jack van der Schyff, a full back who had choked so badly in his previous Test, in 1949, that his kicking duties had been taken over by a prop.

Still, forgive and forget and all that, and Van der Schyff was given another chance to get on the international scoreboard after failing to register a single point in his five previous Tests. This he did with two penalty goals against the Lions, but his defence was shocking. Twice he failed to catch the high ball, letting Jeff Greenwood and Tony O'Reilly in to score tries for the Lions. This gave them a 23-11 lead, but then the Boks bounced back. Two tries were quickly scored and in the third minute of injury time another was scored by Theunis Briers to cut the deficit to 23-22.

The conversion was not especially difficult, halfway between the touch-line and the posts, but South Africa needed it to go over to snatch victory. Instead, Van der Schyff snatched at the kick and pulled it left. His head sank in dejection. The selectors noted not to pick him again.

Asked after the match what he was thinking as Van der Schyff ran in for the kick, O'Reilly gave a clue to the Lions win. "I was merely in communication with the Vatican," he said.

# CHAPTER FIFTEEN

# The Rest of the Worst

# 1    The Warhol look

Stade Français Club Athlétique des Sports Généraux, to give the Paris club its full name, has one of the oldest and most proud histories in French rugby. Founded in 1883, their first championship final was against Racing Club and refereed by Baron Pierre de Coubertin, future founder of the Olympic Games. They have won the French Championship five times since 1998 and were twice runners-up in the Heineken Cup. What a shame, therefore, that Stade are best known for having the most garish, oddest shirts in world rugby.

Blame Max Guazzini, their chairman and a man with an eye for marketing. Thinking that his team's red, white and blue strip was, if patriotic, a bit bland, Guazzini set out to create more identifiable jerseys.

First he started with three flashes of lightning. Then, in 2005, he asked the butch Frenchmen to wear pink. If his players felt like sissies, it worked off the pitch. Guazzini sold 20,000 replica jerseys that season.

Since then he has been determined to keep experimenting – and presumably keep selling. In 2006, a navy blue shirt was presented to the players before their game with Bayonne. It had pink lilies and green flashes all over it and was certainly distinctive. Not quite as distinctive, however, as the shirt revealed for the 2008-09 season which had been inspired by Andy Warhol. It featured metallic blue sleeves and an array of multicoloured images of Blanche de Castille, the Queen of Louis VIII.

Guazzini's marketing plans go beyond mere shirts. He brought in cheerleaders, fireworks and a radio-controlled car to take the tee out to the kicker. He invited the likes of Madonna and Naomi Campbell to matches. He even created a rather homoerotic calendar of his players, called The Gods of Stade. Well it makes a nice change from players being snapped semi-naked in nightclubs.

# Dressing properly for rugby

**M**ax Guazzini (see previous entry) may have been creative but he was not pioneering. French rugby players were wearing silly clothes long before he dressed his Stade Francais team in Marilyn Monroe suits.

Racing Club de France was formed a year before Stade Francais and had a reputation for elitism and being rather toffish. While they dominated the early days of the club game in France with Stade, both sides declined in the 20th century. But in the 1980s players at Racing Club, who called themselves "le show bizz", developed a new philosophy: if they could not be better than other teams, they could at least look better.

Driven by two of their international backs, Franck

Mesnel, the fly half, and Jean-Baptiste Lafond, the wing, Racing Club's antics included playing a game in 1987 against Bayonne while wearing berets. Over the next few years, they wore black make-up, Minstrel-style, against Toulouse, dyed their hair yellow against Béziers and dressed up as pelota players, with white shorts, black jackets and berets, against Biarritz.

To mark the 200th anniversary of the storming of the Bastille in 1989, they wore the historical sans-culottes breeches in the cup semi-final. That was stylish, but not quite as stylish as playing the 1987 final against Toulon wearing pink bow-ties. Although they lost that match, three years later they used the same plan, drank a bottle of champagne on the pitch at half-time – and won.

They were more than just clothes horses, however. Five of the team founded a sportswear company called Eden Park, after the Auckland stadium, which uses a pink bow-tie as its logo. The club became the official formal wear supplier for the France and Wales national teams, proving that sometimes there is a reward in acting the fool.

# 3  Right, that's it. I'm off

In his time as a prop for London Irish – not to mention as a chief superintendent in the Metropolitan Police – George Crawford had seen plenty of foul play, but when he became a referee in the 1980s he was staggered by how much gratuitous violence went on. Eventually he snapped and during a televised match between Bristol and Newport, where the thuggery had become excessive, Crawford stunned the 10,000 crowd and players by just walking off the pitch and letting them get on with it. A local referee had to take over so the match could be completed.

Naturally, the RFU issued a severe reprimand to Crawford, who resigned from the RFU officials' list, but they took no action against the clubs for several weeks until the pressure built from the media. In a scathing article in *The Times* four years later, Crawford attacked the governing body for failing to tackle violence. "I was foolishly of the opinion that the sacrifice [of ending his career by walking off] would be worthwhile," he wrote.

"It is open season for the man in the middle. The newspapers have been full of allegations that referees failed to take control of a number of games as the louts, dressed in the colours of some of the greatest rugby teams in the world, went about their thuggish business. If such behaviour had taken place on a football field, there would have been an inquiry. Instead, what we got was the castigation of the referee."

And it did not end there. Crawford also complained about the way that referees were treated by fans after the game. "How many referees leave clubs totally disillusioned after travelling, in some cases, hundreds of miles to carry out their duties?" he wrote. He went on to call for a mass boycott of rugby matches one Saturday by the referees to force the issue.

How times have changed. Rugby still has its moments of thuggishness, but football appears to have become the sport that puts the standard of the players' behaviour behind the quality of the refereeing. Referees, in the main, get more respect than their counterparts in football, which may have something to do with Crawford's stand.

# 4  What's in a name?

**T**he corporate reality of modern rugby means that clubs and governing bodies have to find ways of raising money wherever they can, but where is their pride or their sense of history when commercialism means a familiar name is erased? Lansdowne Road, in the Ballsbridge district of Dublin, is a name that evokes certain feelings, usually of standing in the rain, awkward lines of sight and the faint smell of urine. But also the old stadium, which opened in 1872, brings memories of fun, gaiety, drinking and playfulness, of the pub in the corner and the train passing under the stand and having to cross the level crossing to get into the stadium.

The new stadium that is being built in Dublin will no doubt be an impressive beast, with excellent facilities for players and spectators alike, but all enthusiasm was killed for the project among many Ireland fans when it was announced that instead of retaining the Lansdowne Road name, the new ground will be called Aviva Stadium to reflect the sponsorship of an insurance company that had itself changed its name from Norwich Union. Hard to see many people kicking up a stink about the death of Norwich Union, however.

Lansdowne Road is not the only famous old name under threat. Eden Park, the Auckland ground where rugby and cricket has been played since 1925, is considering selling its naming rights to raise money before the 2011 World Cup. Frosties Field can only be round the corner. If they want an example of how not to do it, look at Candlestick Park, home of the San Francisco 49ers NFL team, which changed its name to 3Com Park and found the team's fortunes soon declined. How can a crowd get excited about a computer company?

Here's hoping that no more famous rugby grounds take this route and follow the disastrous examples of Heinz Field (home of the Pittsburgh Steelers), a name that suggests playing on baked beans, or Nuremberg FC's EasyCredit Stadion.

# 5   Twelve angry men

Losing a player can often galvanise a team into heroic acts. Being a man down makes everyone else play above themselves. The spirit of camaraderie pulls them through – not to mention the extra space they now have in which to run. But what happens when you lose two or even three players? And what about when that is in a cup final? When do you just give up and realise it won't be your day?

For Moseley, the West Midlands club, those questions were asked in the very first final of what was glamorously called the RFU Club Knock-Out Competition against Gloucester in 1972. This has gone through various sponsorships and is now the EDF Energy Cup. Excitement and tension naturally built before the match and in the first few minutes a series of fights broke out. At the first scrum, Don Lane, the Moseley hooker, stood up after being bitten. The perpetrator, unseen, got away with it. At the second scrum, Nigel Horton, Moseley's international lock, was less lucky. The referee saw him punch Dick Smith on the chin and so Horton was given the record of becoming the first of three (so far) to be sent off in the cup final.

Just before half-time, Moseley were reduced to 13 men when Tom Smith suffered an injury – there were no replacements – and with 20 minutes to go in the second half they were cut to 12 when Ian Pringle, the flanker, also had to limp off. Fifteen against 12 should have been plenty for Gloucester to win, but it took them until injury time, when Mickey Booth and Tom Palmer dropped goals, to be sure of a 17-6 victory. Moseley battled furiously, even though they were playing without a back row, and Gloucester could find no way through or over their stout defence. It was to Moseley's credit that they took the final to the wire, but fans were robbed of a proper spectacle with 15 against 15.

# The Olympic spirit?

**B**y 2016, rugby could be back on the Olympic programme. A meeting of the International Olympic Committee at the end of 2009 will decide whether the sport, in its shortened sevens form, will be readmitted for the first time since the 1924 Games. It is a good pub quiz question to ask who are the reigning champions.

The answer is the United States, who beat France 17-3 in front of 30,000 people at the Stade Colombes near Paris, although the circumstances are rather odd. Only three teams entered for the competition, with France (59-3) and the USA (39-0) both having no difficulty in dispatching Romania, who won the bronze medal despite scoring only one penalty.

The Americans were really a Stanford University

team and there was grouching from the French about their amateur status. Arguments between the sides flared up in the run-in to the final. The US objected to the selection of Admiral Percy Royds, of Great Britain, as referee. A Welshman was chosen instead. In retaliation, France refused to let the US use any practice fields, so the Americans had to practise in a park instead. The French also wouldn't let the Americans film the game and the harmony between the sides was not helped by a break-in to the US dressing room as they trained, with $4,000 stolen while the room was watched by a French attendant.

Despite the bad blood, the bookmakers were making France strong favourites for the final even though the fitter Americans insisted on the game being 45, rather than 40 minutes each way. They were jeered throughout the game, even when the anthems were being played, but gradually the catcalls ceased as the Americans, scoring five tries, showed they could play. The match finished in a near-riot, with one of the American reserves being flattened by a walking stick. Rugby was soon removed from the Olympic programme.

# 7  Twice is two too many

**T**o lose one match is almost regarded as a calamity by most New Zealand fans but to lose twice in a day is beyond the pale. By 1949, the All Blacks nickname, coined on their dominant tour of the northern hemisphere in 1905, was respected around the world but it was not quite feared. South Africa were every bit their equals and when a four-Test series was arranged in the republic New Zealand were determined to send their strongest men, even if the administrators in their wisdom had also arranged a tour to New Zealand by Australia at the same time.

It was a close series, but New Zealand lost all four matches. Having been beaten 15-11 and 12-6 in the first two games, the All Blacks approached the third game in Durban with trepidation, not least because word had already reached them of the fate of their brothers back in the land of the long white cloud.

With 30 men in South Africa, it was very much a third XV who took on Australia in Wellington. They had some talented Maori players in Vince Bevan, Ben Couch and Johnny Smith, who were ineligible on racial grounds to tour South Africa, but in the main these were the fringe players of the All Blacks squad and there were 13 men who made their debuts. Only Smith, the captain, and Couch, the fly half, had pulled on the black shirt before.

Inevitably, they were routed 11-6 and then the game to the west also went against New Zealand, with South Africa sealing a 9-3 win. Australia won the second match of their series and New Zealand were whitewashed 4-0 in South Africa with an 11-8 loss. This time, though, they did not have the ignominy of losing twice in a day. The run of six consecutive losses, though, remains a black period in history for the All Blacks.

# 8  One man too many

**C**live Woodward's approach to winning the 2003 World Cup was to leave no stone unturned, to cover all the bases in his pursuit of the Webb Ellis Cup. Yet the campaign was almost derailed in the pool stage by the failure of his backroom staff to be able to count to 15.

It was the closing stages of England's match against Samoa, a game that they had struggled in at first before winning 35-22, and with Mike Tindall nursing an injury, Dan Luger, it was alleged, ignored the request of the fourth match official to wait for a break in play before replacing his team-mate. Certainly, Luger came on and for six seconds England had 16 men on the pitch before he was ordered off by Jonathan Kaplan, the referee. He even had time to make a tackle. England claimed, however, that because of the official's intransigence they were being expected to play with only 14.

Naturally other sides leapt at the chance to bring England down a peg. Eddie Jones, the Australia coach and a frequent thorn in Woodward's side, got all holier-than-thou. "We all like to stretch protocol to the limit but it's very important that teams follow it," he said. Kaplan probably should have penalised England on the field for their error, but once the match was over the IRB was reportedly considering docking England points.

Woodward had taken a lawyer with him for this eventuality and his arguments, as well as an admission of guilt and an apology, ensured that the only sanction was a £10,000 fine and a ban from the touchline for Dave Reddin, the fitness coach who had tried to send Luger on. England, of course, did not let the row put them off.

In 2008, Queensland Reds complained that referees in the Super 14 turned a blind eye to teams bringing on an extra man. Phil Mooney, their coach, spotted on reviewing the videos that the Sharks had had one man too many on against his side. He was not impressed after being told by the referee that if the Sharks had scored a try with an extra man it would have stood and Queensland would have got a penalty after the re-start. Wonder if that would have been the case had Luger scored in his six seconds of infamy?

# 9   The biggest upsets

**A**nyone who put money on Wales to win the fifth rugby World Cup Sevens in Dubai in 2009 will have made a pretty penny. Not since Samson had his hair cut had Delilah caused such an upset in the Middle East. Wales, 80-1 outsiders before the tournament started, beat Argentina in the final 19-12 to the sound of Tom Jones songs from all corners of the stadium.

If their ultimate victory was unexpected, what was staggering were the results in the four quarter-finals. South Africa, winners of two of that year's four World Series events, lost to Argentina, before Kenya, to the delight of their noisy fans, destroyed Fiji, the defending champions, 26-7. But the biggest shocks were in the matches between Wales and New Zealand and Samoa and England. New Zealand, the perennial champions in the World Series circuit, were taking on a team who had reached one quarter-final in their past four tournaments. New Zealand scored in the first minute, but Lee Williams replied straight away, touching down in the right corner, and Richie Pugh put Wales ahead on the stroke of half-time.

Back came the All Blacks, Lote Raikabula taking an inside pass from Viliame Waqaseduadua to score. The latter, one of New Zealand's best players, had the chance to close out the win two minutes later when he burst through the Wales defence. Alas for New Zealand, as he neared the line, his right knee came up and knocked the ball out of his hands. The All Blacks have choked in World Cups before, but this was silly. With 90 seconds remaining, Tom Isaacs sealed a 15-14 win for Wales, kicking ahead and beating New Zealand's defence.

Samoa, meanwhile, led 21-7 in a thrilling match against England and were 26-19 ahead with 40 seconds remaining and a conversion in front of the posts. The kicker missed it and England had the faintest chance. In fact, the hooter sounded and Samoa jubilantly punted the ball into touch, only for the referee to say there was time for one last play. England moved the ball quickly and Josh Drauniniu slipped through a gap to score. Ben Gollings's conversion took the game into sudden death, which Samoa won. A crazy morning, but fabulous entertainment.

# 10

# A streak of good fortune

I couldn't write a book on bad behaviour at rugby matches without mentioning streakers. As with many of the tales of naughtiness in this book, I don't actually mind streakers at all. They liven up a game and the pleasure of seeing a man – or especially a woman – charge across a freezing pitch in the all together is matched only be seeing them flattened in a tackle by a security guard. It is a great shame that streakers are threatened with fines and imprisonment these days, they add so much to a game. You really have to admire their balls, so to speak.

The two most famous streakers both exhibited their wares at Twickenham. Michael O'Brien, a 25-year-old bearded Australian, had been hitting the Foster's in 1974 and was offered ten pounds by a friend if he could run naked across the pitch and touch the opposite stand. He was caught by the police, who gallantly let him win his bet before cautioning him. O'Brien asked the officer for a kiss, but instead the policeman wisely just offered his helmet to protect O'Brien's modesty. Twenty-five years later, the helmet was auctioned for charity.

The other famous Twickenham streaker was Erica Roe, a bookshop assistant, who whipped off her top and galloped across the turf during a match between England and Australia in 1982, her 40-inch chest mesmerising the crowd as she went. She made £80,000 from TV appearances and modelling after her naked dash.

Finally, two favourite personal memories: the first came in the 1996 Varsity Match on a freezing December afternoon when a female streaker emerged from the South Stand and charged the whole length of the field before being stopped. As the wind whipped across the ground, some wag remarked that if she had been a Light Blue supporter at the start of the chase she would be Dark Blue by the end.

The other occasion was a couple of years ago when Blackheath played the hitherto unbeaten Doncaster in the last game of the season. It was a fabulous day, capped by Blackheath winning 30-0, but the most memorable moment was the male streaker who scampered across the pitch, bits waving willy-nilly, and ran straight into the bar where he could be found, still naked, afterwards having a few merry pints. And no, it wasn't me.

338

# Selected Bibliography

*The Daily Telegraph Chronicle of Rugby*, edited by **Norman Barrett**

*The History of the British and Irish Lions,* **Clem Thomas**

*The Five Nations Story*, **David Hands**

*Classic Rugby Clangers*, **David Mortimer**

*Twickenham,* **Ed Harris**

*Willie John: The Story of My Life,* **Willie John McBride**

*The Times, The Daily Telegraph* and other British and international newspapers

scrum.com, planet-rugby.com, sporting-heroes.net and other websites